Anthropology and Entrepreneurship

THE CURRENT STATE OF RESEARCH AND PRACTICE

*Anthropology and Entrepreneurship Research,
Symposium Proceedings 2020-2021*

Edited by Edward Liebow and Janine Chiappa McKenna
American Anthropological Association

EWING MARION
KAUFFMAN
FOUNDATION

AMERICAN ANTHROPOLOGICAL ASSOCIATION

Anthropology and Entrepreneurship - The Current State of Research and Practice
Edward Liebow and Janine Chiappa McKenna, editors
Published September 2022
CC-BY-NC license

978-1-931303-77-4 (print)
978-1-931303-78-1 (digital)

Published by the American Anthropological Association with generous support
from the Ewing Marion Kauffman Foundation

American Anthropological Association
2300 Clarendon Blvd
Suite 1301
Arlington, VA 22201

Table of Contents

Introduction

The field of anthropology emerged in the nineteenth century as part of a broader critique of the Industrial Revolution and colonial expansion, seeking to make sense of the ways in which economic and technological changes had fundamentally altered livelihoods, family arrangements, communities, political institutions, and the patterns of values and beliefs that reinforce and perpetuate the social and geopolitical order. Anthropological research and its applications have largely been motivated by underlying interests in calling out the root causes of social injustice and unsustainable resource use.

One consistent and timely research thread in anthropology's intellectual history is the examination of entrepreneurship, especially in industrial and post-colonial economies. Thanks to the generous support of the Ewing Marion Kauffman Foundation, the American Anthropological Association (AAA) has been able to recognize some exemplary scholarship on anthropology and entrepreneurship through a series Annual Meeting symposia held in 2020 and 2021.

For this symposium series, AAA has sought a mix of papers based on research from around the world, not just North America. AAA has been especially interested in highlighting research that has direct practical application in business and entrepreneurship and that addresses solutions to pressing environmental, economic and social problems. Among the research areas of particular interest are: (1) entrepreneurial behavior and the social, cultural, and economic institutions that facilitate the emergence and ongoing support of such behavior; (2) innovative approaches to entrepreneurship training and development; (3) partnerships and financial instruments that support new enterprises; and (4) innovative approaches to enterprises that explicitly aim to serve public interests and/or urgent social needs.

Symposium papers have been chosen from among extended proposals by a panel of business anthropologists including Ken Erickson (U South Carolina), Kyle Gibson (Facebook), Susan Kresnicka (KRI and Associates), Timothy deWaal Malefyt (Fordham U), and Inga Treitler (Anthropological Imagination, LLC). The panel has been especially interested in data-rich accounts drawn from ethnographic research, mixed-methods research, and case studies. Bearing in mind the problems faced by small enterprises, downsizing businesses, franchise models, and of enterprises across different sectors of the economy, proposals have addressed a wide range of urgent questions like succession in family business, no-growth companies, startup culture, innovative approaches to credit and capital formation, informal economy, and public/private partnerships. The current volume offers a selection of the papers presented in the 2020 and 2021 symposia, along with a summary of a conversation the 2021 authors had with symposium moderator and business anthropologist Patricia Sunderland.

First is Worku Nida's paper on the rise to enterprising dominance of an Ethiopian ethnic group, the Gurage. The Gurage case in contemporary Ethiopia is important because it follows the historical arc of a once-marginalized ethnic group, which, over several generations in the twentieth century, went from being farmers pushed off their rural lands and forced to move to urban areas, ascending to a dominant role in nearly every sector of the Ethiopian economy. Nida asks why this group has enjoyed singular success, where other groups in Ethiopia disadvantaged by the nation-building project did not. Three elements are key:

(1) **Group living** – forced by necessity into group enclaves, the Gurage saw group living circumstances as an opportunity to pool their resources with collective savings and revolving credit arrangements, exchange information about working strategies, and forming an expandable labor pool that could be mobilized as needed.

(2) **Links to global capitalism** – with other avenues among Ethiopians cut off and forced to turn outward, ties to colonial powers and transnational merchants gained the Gurage access to investment capital and markets that have led to large-scale success.

(3) **State supports** – the creation of banks and the modern taxation system led the way to replacing expat companies, especially coffee companies, with Ethiopian companies, which could succeed and weather the socialist push towards nationalization because of the formation of state banks.

Atak Ayaz presents his work on Turkey's enterprising artisanal wine producers. Ayaz points out that winemaking had become a nation-building project after the establishment of Turkey's secular government in 1923 and benefitted from significant state-led investments. In recent years, an artisanal wine-producing sector, what Ayaz terms "post-industrial," has developed to meet the growing market of upwardly mobile urban consumers and affirm their identification with small-scale, high-quality, local production. Although some of the "post-industrial" enterprises rely on investors, most have been supported through family money and are guided by foreign-trained family members or international wine consultants. This emerging class of vintners have altered their lifestyles, establishing new life in the localities to which they have shifted their capital. While long-term residents or rural areas are abandoning agriculture as it becomes less economically viable, well-educated urbanites are modifying the pastoral landscape. This connection to the countryside adds an important dimension to internal migration patterns, and a shift in urban/rural distinctions in social stratification and inequality.

Riddhi Bhandari has a timely piece about the pandemic's impacts on entrepreneurs in the tourism industry in Agra (home of the Taj Mahal). He notes that for small-scale tour operators, the years immediately preceding the pandemic's start had helped achieve stability through steady growth in client bookings and reputation. As in many places, their start-up enterprises had depended on other earners in the family to dampen income volatility. After the initial lockdown, the composition of visitor population changed, with fewer international visitors and visitors from the region booking shorter stays, and fewer purchases made locally. Relief from taxes, rent, and utility bills was difficult to find, loans rather than grants were on offer, and the State used the post-lockdown phase as an opportunity to experiment with additional restrictions (caps on visitor volume, regulation of tour guides, online-only ticketing) that were harmful in the short term. Being readily adaptable, however, entrepreneurs in the local area are always looking for their next venture, and they see the possibility of synergies with other tourist attractions that will make their businesses more sustainable. State leadership in addressing pollution, enhancing infrastructure, and providing direct income subsidies would help reduce risk and uncertainty.

Lora Koycheva shares some of her observations on startups and academic partnerships with the private sector in Europe, along with an argument for how anthropological research can complement work on entrepreneurship from other disciplines. She points out that research on entrepreneurship has often focused on the characteristics of successful individuals, e.g., the entrepreneurial "mindset," with relatively little emphasis on the contextual factors that make or break entrepreneurial success. Even when examining institutional climate, the outcome variables have emphasized individual behavior. Context makes all the difference, Koycheva argues, and case studies of "make-a-thons" as well as university partnerships with the private sector highlight key cultural elements that should be cultivated and nurtured. "Make-a-thons" are time-pressured formats for collaborating on the development of mechanical (rather than digital) prototypes. The have a playful orientation, and involve small groups gathering and then disbanding quickly after they are over. The creative underpinnings of innovation on display, i.e., what it takes to be an entrepreneur in a setting of open, unstructured, improvisational and messy experimentation: "fake it until you make it," "fail fast and often," and "better to ask for forgiveness than for permission." How to create and stimulate startup culture in the academic context has great relevance for creating novel approaches to entrepreneurship training and development and more broadly for the potential of spinning off companies rooted in scientific research. Academic and business orientations to "research" – the former being characterized by "disciplined rule followers" and the latter by "playful rule breakers." The fact that we see individuals with similar mindsets (resilient, visionary, persistent) and similar practices (pitching strategies, iterating on the original idea) result in different outcomes suggests that we ought to focus as much on context as "mindset" in characterizing the academic venturing sector.

Angela VandenBroek reflects on the use of "hype storytelling" as she observed it at a well-known Swedish pitch event series, providing for us a peek behind the curtain into the process for pitching venture capitalists (VCs) to persuade them to invest in startup entrepreneurs. She notes that "hype" storytelling in a VC pitch must avoid the perception of cynical aggrandizement that goes against Swedish social norms and be directed instead at the VCs' needs. In other words, one must avoid creating the perception that one is motivated by a glamorous lifestyle and emphasize instead the personal struggles, sacrifices, and ambitions for social rather than personal benefit. The pitch ought to set forward a vision of a better future to work toward, rather than a fabricated lie that is meant to defraud and deceive. One need not believe that the hyped claims will definitely be achieved, only that they credibly could happen. As VandenBroek points out, VCs have a widely shared vision of success, what Steve Blank calls the scalable startup. Hype storytelling that registers with VCs, then, foreground the VCs' values and needs with claims like "addicting" technology, large paying user bases, and "social stuff." These VC-friendly characteristics of hype don't necessarily attract diverse allies to provide alternative financial, material, or political support. VandenBroek closes with a thought-provoking question regarding how space might be created for alternative narratives that feature credible futures for diverse allies, creating new possibilities for the purposes of start-ups, how they should operate, and what their priorities ought to be?

The last paper in the collection, by Jamie Wong, is derived from extensive case studies in Shenzen (China), also focusing on the relationship between entrepreneurs and the VCs to which they turn for funding. She examines the underlying social fabric that is the foundation of what she calls "growth hacking." Wong observes that to grow their enterprises in the fastest way possible, startups seek leverage from VC funding and by outsourcing their operations like computer programming, design, and manufacturing. Chasing growth at such a pace, a "gyroscope-like" economy is created that cannot balance unless it keeps spinning rapidly. Leverage is often gained by promises of performance that are deemed credible because of the organization that vouches for them; if a large, well-established player in the marketplace indicates that it sees promise, its reputation may be sufficient to attract further investors, a self-compounding virtuous cycle. Wong also observes that leverage does not accumulate smoothly over time. Instead, its accumulation resembles the scaling of boulders, whereby points of contact momentarily serve to leverage the climber upwards. Most importantly, beneath the sheen of novelty and hype, the VC model is based on recognized processes of establishing and maintaining social ties, which have been rebranded as "growth hacking."

Some thematic lines appear in this collection, especially the role of the state in supporting entrepreneurship, cooperation and competition in entrepreneurial development, scale of enterprise, timeframes for sustaining innovations, and the special role anthropological methods can play in illuminating the social and institutional context of entrepreneurship. These and more specific issues raised in some of the papers are explored further in a conversation that was part of the 2021 symposium, moderated by Patricia Sunderland.

The AAA is grateful for the generous support of the Ewing Marion Kauffman Foundation, and especially to Program Officer Lara Arnold, for making this symposium series possible.

Edward Liebow
AAA Executive Director
May 2022

African Entrepreneurialsm: The Emergence of Ethiopian Gurage Entrepreneurs as a National Capitalist Class

WORKU NIDA, University of California, Riverside

Introduction

Entrepreneurialism[1] plays a critical role in developing countries because of its power to propel economic development. It is particularly significant in Africa given various scholars refer to the continent as being "less developed" than the West (Rodney 1983, Ferguson 1994, Moyo 2009). The Ethiopian Gurage represent an important case in this respect. The ethnic Gurage transformed themselves from subsistence agriculturalists and serfs into owners and managers of major business enterprises. This chapter examines some of the key processes by which the once-underclass Gurage emerged as a new entrepreneurial class in Ethiopia over the last seven decades. It draws on two years of ethnographic fieldwork and extensive historical research.

The modern country of Ethiopia resulted mainly from Emperor Menilek II's imperial campaigns during the second half of the nineteenth century. These campaigns resulted in the previously subsistence agriculturalist Gurage, along with several other groups, being dispossessed of their lands, and subjected to serfdom (Shack 1966, Nida 1991). The dispossession triggered Gurage movements to Addis Ababa and other urban areas, providing the basis for Gurage entrepreneurialism. Currently, these Gurage migrant-turned-entrepreneurs play leading roles in import and export trades, manufacturing, wholasling, and distribution, retailing, real estate, and service industries.

This is part of a larger study based on the analysis of stories told by pioneer, second, and third generation Gurage entrepreneurs as well as their descendants in explaining their entrepreneurial success. Sixty in-depth interviews demonstrate key Gurage entrepreneurial patterns:

---

[1] Entrepreneurship is the most widely used term in the topical studies. Instead, I use the term entrepreneurialism to emphasis the agentive aspect of the process, through which people make both money and identity entrepreneurially.

Many started with little capital and working through entrepreneurial paths such as shoeshining, street vending, stand-owning, kiosk-owning, and shopkeepers but were eventually able to accumulate enough capital to build large businesses such as hotels, restaurants, manufacturing firms, and import-export trades. By working as employees for expatriate firms, many Gurage gained the experiences and networks to run their own businesses in various fields.

A larger study, of which this chapter is a part, explains the Gurage transformation from serfs to a national bourgeoisie by analyzing what I call a three-legged entrepreneurial scaffolding. It involves three variables: a) personal attributes, b) ethnic and cultural resources, and c) the political/structural resources (including state support as well as their mentorship by the expatriates). I focus here on two of these key variables, personal attributes, and ethnic-cultural resources with special emphasis on *fano* (or migrant group living) and *equbs* (Gurage rotating saving and credit associations).

Situating the Gurage in Ethiopia and Entrepreneurial Studies

The Gurage are one of the eighty-six ethnic groups that constitute a multiethnic and multicultural nation, Ethiopia, an ancient country with a rich history of global ties. It is located in the Horn of Africa, bordered by Djibouti in the east, Somalia in the southeast, Kenya in the south, Sudan in the west, and Eritrea in the north and northeast. The current total population is estimated at 120 million in 2022, 85 percent of which are rural residents. Agriculture generates 52 percent of Ethiopia's gross domestic product (Central Statistical Authority 1999).

The agrarian Gurage inhabit Gurage land, which is located in the southwestern part of Ethiopia, about 200 kilometers south and southwest of Addis Ababa. Sedentary agriculture, farming, raising livestock, and trade constituted the major economic activities for the Gurage. The cultivation of *ensete ventricosum*, their staple food crop, is a major part of rural Gurage life.[2] The Gurage are adherents of Christianity (including Orthodox, Catholic, Protestant, and Pentecostal), Islam, and a variety of traditional religions (Nida 1990, 1993; Shack 1966, 1976).

A crucial aspect of Gurage social history is Gurage resistance[3] to Emperor Menilek II's imperial conquests.[4] Their fourteen years of resistance ended at the battle of Jebidu in 1888. The Gurage lost the battle and their independence and lands with it, resulting in harsh treatment and heavy tributes imposed on the Gurage by the Amhara-dominated ruling nobility. A large number of the Gurage resisted such atrocities with their feet. The contexts of Menilek's conquests and the resultant migration put the Gurage in contact with a wide range of Ethiopian and expatriate groups, through which they encountered global capitalism. They established new relationships with other Ethiopians and expatriate business people, first as laborers and then as entrepreneurs. The Gurage entered and dominated Addis Ababa's labor markets, and people began to associate Gurageness with early Gurage engagement in menial labor (working as porters and shoeshiners, making and selling ropes) and trade (selling skins and hides). For example, the Indian word *cooli* became synonymous with Gurage as people hailed "Gurage! Gurage!" to call out for porters in Addis. Further, they worked for Ethiopian nobility, traders, and foreigners such as the Arabs, Indians, French, Greeks, Armenians, and Italians.

---

2 *Ensete ventricosum*, also known as false banana, is the main staple food crop for about 20 million Ethiopians, living in the southwestern parts of contemporary Ethiopia, the Gurage included. Shack (1966:3) dubbed these parts of the country as 'the ensete complex areas.'

3 The Soddo group, however, submitted to Menilek's forces peacefully in 1876.

4 Similarly, other communities including, Hadiya, Kambata, Sidama, Gamu, Waliyata, and a number of Oromo groups such as Kaffa and Arsi were victims of those campaigns.

Through such encounters, many Gurage apprenticed and evolved as successful entrepreneurs, replacing the expatriate business people who dominated Ethiopia's commercial sector (Temtime 1995; Nida 1996, 2006).

A major question in studies of entrepreneurship concerns the different levels of capitalist entrepreneurial success among both groups and individuals. Two major and overlapping theoretical streams dominate. Inspired by Weber ([1904] 1992), cultural theories focus on cultural ideas and values (Barth 1962, Light and Gold 2000, Butler 2005, Jalloh 1999, Rutashobya 1998). For example, Weber attributed the rise and development of modern entrepreneurship to a work ethic of Calvinistic Protestantism. Structural theories explain entrepreneurial development in terms of class, social networks, and ethnic and kin solidarities (Bonacich 1973, Aldrich and Waldinger 1990, Portes and Bach 1985, Beresford 2020).

My analysis of Gurage entrepreneurialism draws from both theoretical streams and goes beyond them by rethinking entrepreneurialism as a simultaneously money- and identity-making process and by highlighting the dialectical relationship between entrepreneurial success and (ethnic) identity. Rooted in the history of their fourteen years of resistance against emperor Menelik II's territorial expansionist campaigns (Nida 1991, 2006, Bonsa 1997), Gurage migrations and entrepreneurialism emerged as forms of both Gurage resistance against and contributions to the emergent imperial-state, playing a crucial part in modern Ethiopian nation- and city-making projects. I view entrepreneurialism as a self-crafting, self-transforming, and liberating enterprise, with the aim to show the relationship between entrepreneurialism, identity, and social change.

The Nexus of the Personal, Ethnic-Cultural, and Structural in Gurage Entrepreneurial Success

Gurage entrepreneurs transformed themselves from *gebars* (an Amharic word for tribute payers) into urban employees and then into owners and managers of successful business enterprises, becoming an Ethiopian capitalist class. The national contexts for Gurage entrepreneurialism were created by the rise of Menilek II's empire, the Gurage conquest in 1888, their resultant migration,[5] and urbanization, especially the development of Addis Ababa as the capital city of modern Ethiopia. These structural forces and their encounters with the global capitalism created what Tarrow (1998, 144, 163) calls "political opportunities" for Gurage entrepreneurialism.

A dialectical interplay between the personal, cultural, and structural forces supported Gurage entrepreneurial success and their rise as a national bourgeois. Relying on kinship and ethnicity as cooperative ties for entrepreneurial purposes, and developing other people's associations of trade with Gurage, created an ethnically Gurage-dominated business network with an initial foothold in a few business sectors that provided a base for later expanding those enterprises. Gurage entrepreneurialism signifies an ideology of cultural fit and fitness for entrepreneurial success.

Through their entrepreneurial practices, the Gurage created institutions such as *equb* (Gurage rotating savings and credit associations), within and through which personal attributes such as working hard attained cultural forms *and* the personal, cultural, and structural interplayed with and co-constituted one another. This particular orientation created an ideol-

---

5 The Gurage are known for their large-scale migration as revealed in the national Amharic proverb: *Guragena landrover yemidersubet yelem*, that is, "There is no place where the Gurage and Land Rover do not reach." For more on this topic, see Nida 2006.

ogy of ethnic entrepreneurialism that rendered Gurage entrepreneurial fields as male, though subsequently, Gurage women made significant contributions.

Zemzem Gherbi was a successful Gurage woman entrepreneur emerging from street vending to owner and manager of several retail, wholesale, distribution, import-export, and real estate businesses and a big hotel in the Merkato, the main market area in Addis Ababa. Zemzem was born in Addis Ababa in 1918 and died in 2000. The local English weekly, *Addis Tribune*, described Zemzem as "the workaholic lady" who turned upside down "some fettering social and traditional business taboos" and played a major role in transforming the image of the Merkato.[6]

More female entrepreneurs emerged within the second and third generations of Gurage entrepreneurs. Fessesu, 42, a successful woman entrepreneur from Geto, began by selling *kitfo* (minted and spiced meat), a Gurage specialty. This is typical of Gurage women entrepreneurs who commercialized aspects of their ethnicity through marketing Gurage food specialties. Similarly, Mulu, 68, a female hotelier from Chaha, emerged from small and labor-intensive activities. She started by "selling *qolo* (roasted barely), peanuts, and boiled corn as well as beans on the streets during the day and at a *tej* (honey wine)-house in the evenings, from which I saved some money which I used to start my *kitfo* business" (interview, Addis Ababa, November 17, 2002).

Most successful Gurage entrepreneurs partially attributed their successes to their personal attributes including: hardworking qualities (getting up early and working long hours); willingness to do menial and manual jobs; savings programs including refraining from extravagant expenditures such as paying many visits to the villages, or consuming expensive foods and drinks such as beer and whiskey; using their savings productively; avoiding vacations; and employing profitable purchasing strategies such as being willing to travel to distant places to buy items. These constitute the first leg of the entrepreneurial scaffolding.

Zeni, 44, a successful Gurage women respondent from Ezha, who entered the business world in the 1980s, explains why she has succeeded:

> I think it is because of my efforts. Becoming successful takes your own efforts. You have to work hard and I did. I did everything I could. I worked as cook in the kitchen, as a waitress serving my customers, as a manager of my restaurants, as a purchaser of items needed for my businesses. What didn't I do? I sold *qolo* [roasted barley] on the streets and at my high school, which I started with five birr [US$2.50 in 1981]. I started a contraband trade, from which I saved small capital to start my first small *kitfo* business in the Merkato in 1981, where I worked late and I even slept on a wooden-cutting board that I used to make *kitfo*. I got up at 4:00 a.m. in the morning to go to Burayo [in the outskirt of Addis Ababa] to buy good quality meat for cheaper prices. Then I didn't even have my own car. I had to carry the meat from the butchery houses to the taxi stop in Burayo and back in the Merkato, from the taxi station to my restaurant. I lived a very stressful life then. Thanks to God, I am not living it now; here I am running my own restaurant, real estate, and retail businesses and doing really well (interview, Addis Ababa, March 13, 2004).

The Ethnic-Cultural Institutionalization of the Personal

In this section, I explore the *social* implications of the Gurage use of elements of their ethnic-culture entrepreneurially. These elements are tools that constitute the second leg of the scaffolding and provide a competitive edge to the Gurage in relation to others. These tools

---

6   https://allafrica.com/stories/200112100499.html (accessed April 6, 2022)

include *fano* group life and *equbs*, which have served as major breeding grounds and tools for spreading Gurage entrepreneurial ideologies. The successful three generations of Gurage entrepreneurs that I interviewed harnessed aspects of their ethnic and kin ties as resources in building and expanding their business enterprises.

Fano group life: Gurage migrants led a group life of ten to twenty persons sharing a room known in Gurage as *yefano nibiret* in urban settings. A group of five to twelve persons sharing a room is still being practiced by many Gurage migrants.[7] Many of the elderly Gurage entrepreneurs recounted how they began by working for and living in the *fano* houses. Agaz Girma, from Geto subgroup, explains the significance of *fano* group living:

> When I first came to Addis Ababa as a young boy, I lived in a *fano* house where my father lived with fourteen others who were also from the same area, and some of them were my paternal relatives. I did domestic work in the house. That is how we started back then. I made coffee and tea, which I served them with bread. I fetched water. I cleaned the house. Later, I learnt how to make *shiro wot* [stew from pea flour]. I bought *enjera* [pancake-like bread] from *gulit* [small open neighborhood markets] and bread from Arab shops for them. I was eating and sleeping there, without paying a rent. I saved my salary, which I later used to start shoeshine and lottery-selling businesses. My father also gave me some money. This was the foundation. Living there was decisive. That is where I learnt about all kinds of business ideas. You know, everybody talked about what they did, and how much they gained every evening. I was listening to their inspiring stories. Besides, I was living with my relatives, with my father, and with people I knew from the village. In a sense, it felt like I was in the village. You know, because of that nobody treats you badly. That is how our fathers lived and that is how we followed their footsteps (interview, Addis Ababa, October 12, 2004).

Group living had crucial implications for Gurage entrepreneurial successes. First, economically, is savings. The *fano* group life enabled them to live cheaply and to save money, some of which they used as seed money for initiating and developing their own business enterprises. They used their savings for other purposes as well, such as helping and visiting rural kin. Such assistance was a kind of entrepreneurial investment, as exchanges of gifts and frequent visits sustained and nurtured their kin and ethnic networks, and also encouraged further migration for the development of Gurage entrepreneurialism.

Second, group living emerged as vital fora where they shared and exchanged information about their daily life experiences, jobs, businesses, and what was going on in their specific social worlds within the city, as well as concerns about their agrarian families. In other words, the group living experience constituted an important way in which shared agendas and ideologies (both subgroup-specific and pan-Gurage ones) were formed, mediated, and communicated to numerous members of urban and rural Gurage communities.

Third, socially, *fano* living was (and still is) collaboration at work. As Agaz describes above, by living together with their close family members and kin in strange urban settings, they created intimate networks within which they were engaged in a joint project of translating the unfamiliar into the familiar and the vice versa. This practice enabled them to recarve parts

---

7   Such group life is also common among the entrepreneurial groups including Japanese, Chinese, and Jews in the United States, the Indians in Britain, East and South Africa, the Yemeni Arabs in Ethiopia, as well as other African groups in Africa cities (Bonacich and Modell 1981, Jalloh 1999).

of the city's terrain in their own terms.[8] Group living provided them with shared goals and ideologies, a sense of social well-being, of living in an intimate, friendly and family-oriented environment, and, thus, of stability. Such emotional feelings would play a major role in creating individual and collective self-confidence in Gurage migrants, and in helping them succeed. Group living served as a social arena where a distinct sense of becoming and being *entrepreneurial* Gurage—an ideology of ethnic entrepreneurialism—was (re)produced. Fourth, group living attracted new immigrants from the villages, and served as an important supply of new labor force for established and wealthy Gurage entrepreneurs.

The distinct sense of becoming and being entrepreneurial Gurage was further reinforced by others' perceptions of Gurage group living. During the first five decades of Gurage migration, some landlords resisted renting their places to Gurage tenants because of their views of Gurage as "disgusting and unclean." The landlords, dominated by the Amharas, did not like the Gurage ways of living in a large group.

Elderly Gurage entrepreneurs had their own politically charged opinions of the Amhara landlords as "showy and pretentious," invoking their labor contribution to the development of Addis Ababa as the nation's modern capital city. "Whose sweat and labor built Addis Ababa, the city they [Amhara] claim to own? It is we who built Addis Ababa, and in the city we made, they were unwilling to rent us their houses," said Wolde, 76, an entrepreneur from the Chaha subgroup. The Gurage also interjected their agrarian experiences into their counter-discourses where they compared and contrasted "beautiful Gurage *jefore* [i.e., village settlement patterns] and architecture" with that of the Amhara village settings and houses. "They thought they knew about beauty, and that we do not. However, the contrary is true given that the Amhara live in far inferior houses and settings to those of Gurage, on all fronts. Our beautiful *jefore* themselves are like towns," said Agaz Girma. The Gurage reframe the story and describe themselves as the main builders of Addis Ababa (and Ethiopia), re-carving its urban space for commercial and residential uses, and creating their own ethnic-turned-national urban aesthetic.

Equbs: Gurage Rotating Savings and Credit Associations9

Equb played crucial roles in Gurage entrepreneurial success. It served the Gurage as shorthand for sticking together, it generated otherwise scarce capital, it provided an organizational structure and ideology, and it constituted one of the major forms of social mobilization in Gurage entrepreneurialism. In serving these and other entrepreneurially important purposes, *equb* has entailed a double-edged nature of mentoring as both helping and exploiting kin and co-ethnics by successful entrepreneurs.

Rotating savings and credit associations are ubiquitous in Africa, Asia, Latin America, and their diasporas in Europe, the Americas, and the Caribbean. Social scientists have long been interested in understanding these institutions and they have generated abundant literature on various aspects of them in a variety of sociocultural settings (Ardener and Burman

---

8 That is, by recreating their own places named after their sub regions such as Chaha *safar* (area or neighborhood), Muher *safar*, Ezha *safar*, Soddo *safar*, Enor *safar*, Dobi *safar*, Gejja *safar*, and Sore Amba. On the history of other Safars in Addis Ababa, see Bahru 1987.

9 Ardener defines rotating savings and credit associations in a fairly comprehensive manner as, "an association formed upon a core of participants who make regular contributions to a fund which is given in whole or in part to each contributor in turn" (1995, 1). For example, the Gurage use *equbs* where members create an association and contribute an agreed upon amount of money every week or month, and members take turns to use the lump sum of the contributions to build or expand businesses.

1995; Geertz 1963; Light and Gold 2000). Rotating savings and credit associations serve two central functions, savings and credit, although writers emphasized various aspects of these institutions.

Equbs are the Gurage-turned-Ethiopian versions of rotating savings and credit associations. *Equbs* constitute important aspects of Gurage ethnicity and culture that have been harnessed for entrepreneurial purposes, playing an instrumental role in Gurage entrepreneurial development. Historically, *equbs* were Gurage village women's innovation used to bring resources such as milk, butter, and money for annual festivities and weddings.[10] Later, these institutions proved their elasticity in urban settings, where Gurage migrants used them in new ways. In the context of Ethiopia, thus, *equbs* are Gurage innovations.[11]

I asked my respondents about the source of their capital to initiate and expand businesses, and their answers included *equbs*, family resources, loans from friends and kin, and bank loans (especially after they reached at certain stage of success so that they could have collateral). *Equbs* were by far the most commonly cited resource of entrepreneurial capital for the three generations of Gurage entrepreneurs. "You would not find a single real Gurage who became wealthy without [using] equb," said Desalegn, a male entrepreneur from Ezha. "At some stage in our lives, we all used equb," said Kassa, a male entrepreneur from Gumer subgroup. *"We all are children of equb* [emphasis mine]," confirmed Sirgaga, another male key respondent and leading manufacturer from Silte subgroup. Mulu, a female respondent and successful hotelier from the Chaha subgroup said, "equb is our [Gurage's] liberator. To get bank loans, you have to become somebody. Equb is what makes us reach that level of somebody. Once you are somebody, banks are willing to lend you money."

These messages and views of *equbs* are nowhere better captured than in a national Amharic saying: "*sewen sew yaderegew equb new*," (i.e., "*equb* makes man [people]"). This particular national proverb emerged as Gurage entrepreneurs' counter-slogan to the hegemonic discourses of the "socialist" Derge state in the 1970s, which were anti-private, capitalist economic sector. One of the socialist slogans was Engel's famous quote: "*sewen sew yaderegew sira new*," (i.e., "labor makes man [people])," to which Gurage entrepreneurs responded with their own slogan, a proverb that became national. *Equbs* not only helped Gurage achieve demographic and leadership superiority within the national entrepreneurial landscape, but also constituted a major mechanism through which Ethiopians and Ethiopianness become Guragized.

Equbs have played crucial organizational and ideological roles in successful Gurage entrepreneurialism. *Equbs* are coalitions of Gurage and non-Gurage Ethiopians with similar (mostly entrepreneurial) ideologies and goals whose members pool their resources and function collectively as well as individually. Practiced in a variety of sociocultural settings, *equbs* come in multiple forms, shapes, and sizes. There are three local categories of *equb*: small, medium, and large, defined in terms of the amount of weekly investment, the lump sum contributions, and the number of members. The large *equbs* are organized by experienced (usually elderly) successful entrepreneurs, and their members are mostly wealthy, with lump sum contributions between 200,000-500,000 Ethiopian birr (about U.S. $3,914-$9,784 in 2022). In contrast, small *equbs* are organized by young beginners ranging from street vendors and shoeshine boys to shopkeepers and owners of small businesses, and their contributions range from fifty cents a

---

[10] Parallel stories of rotating savings and credit associations' evolution from women's activities are reported elsewhere (see Ardener and Burman 1995, particularly chapter 10, Raji Mohini Sethi's report on Indian *chit*).

[11] Also, see Pankhurst and Eshete (1956) and Aredo 1991.

day for shoeshine boys to fifty birr a week for shopkeepers and others. Everything between the small and large ones are referred to as medium *equbs*. Some associations are specific to certain class, age, gender, or subregion.

There are three crucial yardsticks that are commonly held by the leaders and members of *equbs* to assess their success. *Equbs* are measured by the number of members recruited into the associations, by completing the associations' business with little or no incidence of fraud, and by the number of members (mostly entrepreneurs) they help succeed. The *equb* leaders work hard and compete with each other because they gain several crucial benefits from their position including receiving one lump sum payment of *equb* for free, having priorities on getting the lump sum, and decision-making powers. In this sense, *equbs* themselves are businesses, functioning at once as profit-making and collaborative mechanisms. Organizing and leading *equbs* is a way of helping others while simultaneously making business, and it is the business side of *equbs* that sustain them as significant institutions within Gurage entrepreneurialism.

Equbs leaders and members perform the double-edged function of mentoring as helping and exploiting kin and co-ethnics. *Equb* leaders compete for "good" members because the quality of members is directly related to *equb* and business success. Thus, *equb* shows some of the ways in which individual interests and group interests coexist and co-constitute one another. It is an entrepreneurial *rewriting* of structures (ethnic and family ties) and cultures and at the same time a reconstituting of *equb* as a business enterprise. The *equb* leader's personal desires can be fulfilled if he or she is capable of serving other members' interests. The theoretical significance is that individual desires are socially and historically constituted even within the capitalist entrepreneurial fields, which are usually assumed to be defined by "individualism."

During my field work, I observed two equb meetings held weekly on Sundays organized and led by Tenkir Teni and Kibru Melese. As a young entrepreneur, Tenkir's *equb* was considered to be small, with 60,000 Ethiopian birr (about U.S. $1,174 in 2022) lump sum weekly contribution, in contrast to Kibru's large *equb* with 250,000 Ethiopian birr (roughly U.S. $4,892 in 2022). Kibru has organized and led a number of *equbs* since 1970. My observation and interview materials reveal that being an ethnic Gurage alone is not a sufficient condition to access ethnic resources such as *equbs*. In order to be able to use *equbs*, one has to be a good member. I asked Kibru to define a "good" *equb* member. He explained:

> A good [*equb*] member is one who is trustworthy, who works hard, pays his [her] weekly contributions on time and without any interruption, and one who can complete the payment without any fraud. Also, a good member is a person who uses his [her] *equb* [lump sum money] wisely.

The existence of *equbs* takes place within the context of power relations and power struggles between the leaders and their followers, where both accommodation and resistance are part of the *equb* life process. Thus, *equbs* are the sites for power struggles signifying an (entrepreneurial) *ideological* reconstitution of social (especially, kinship) bases of economic adaptations within urban capitalist relations of production. Since Gurage migrant-turned-entrepreneurs found themselves living and working in new, urban settings that intersected with the emergent national market economy and global capitalism, they rewrote *equb*, initially a village Gurage institution, as a capitalist enterprise through their migratory experiences and their encounters with capitalism. *Equb* became a site where global capitalism, Gurageness, and Ethiopianness intersected and co-constituted one another. As a result, the parameters of participation in *equbs* are no longer decided just on the basis of kinship or ethnicity,[12] as it now involves a new dynamic of membership, sharing and exclusion, as well as cooperation and competition.

Equbs as disciplinary tools

The *equbs* constitute *forms* of Gurage self-organization and self-disciplining or policing. Most, if not all, Gurage entrepreneurs and enterprises belonged to one or another *equb* association at one point in their histories. Almost every member entrepreneur attends the *equb* meetings, where administrative business such as who pays or does not pay their contributions properly is revealed to the public. The *equb* meetings manage some degree of institutional and organizational transparency.

After the 1990s, due to the increase in their size with budgets ranging between 200,000 and 500,000 birr (about U.S. $3,911-$9,780 in 2022) *equbs'* stakes also increased and were seriously organized. For example, each *equb* appoints its own lawyer to attend to legal matters and protect the association legally and follows strict rules and regulations such as requiring a member to have four members as guarantees at the receipt of their *equb* lump sum. Thus, *equb* members are expected to be disciplined, paying their contributions in a timely manner and in full. With such associational openness, the mere threat of labeling and stigma motivates members to fulfill their membership obligations to *equbs*, to which the members' access is crucial, especially in the absence of formal institutional support of mechanisms such as bank loans and prior entrepreneurial family resources or capital to draw on.

Many informants highlight such disciplinary roles of equbs. For example, Zeni narrates as follows:

> *Equb* … has another advantage [in addition to being a source of capital]. *It disciplines you as an entrepreneur and a member of a community* [emphasis added]. The good thing about taking an *equb* pay out early is that once you take the money you are in debt. You owe a huge amount of money which you have to pay back. In order to do that you have to be disciplined, working hard and avoiding unnecessary expenses. Being in debt motivates you to work hard because you want to pay your debt and keep your good name. Otherwise, there is nowhere to turn to when you need equb or other kinds of help from others (interview, Addis Ababa, March 13, 2004).

Various *equb* narratives illuminate that *equbs* provide participants with a sense of duty or calling that deeply resonates with Weber's (1992) notion of Calvinist asceticism, which, he argued, provided a unique religiously based practical ethics for the development of the "new spirit" of capitalism in Europe.

As a result of Gurage migratory and entrepreneurial experiences, the meaning and uses of *equb* changed from a village Gurage women's local institution to an important urban Gurage capitalist mechanism of generating capital for investment. Also, *equbs* as educational and disciplinary fora performed Calvinistically in that they produced a sense of calling and (re)

---

12   Due to their new capitalist roles, *equbs* in urban settings have become so flexible that non-Gurage individuals are accepted as members of *equbs* that are led and dominated by Gurage entrepreneurs. It has become common for many Gurage *equbs* both at home and abroad to include considerable non-Gurage members.

instilled individual agency. In contrast to Weber's assertion that such senses (work ethics) can only emerge from Calvinism, the Gurage data show that notions of calling come in different shapes and forms, emanating from varied sources such as the institutions of *equb*, which signify the cultural and structural foundations of Gurage entrepreneurialism.[13]

Without such disciplinary roles, *equbs* could rapidly exacerbate the entrepreneurial problems they were meant to solve. Various stories emphasize that accessing *equbs* is a necessary but not a sufficient factor, in producing entrepreneurial success. When *equbs* are used unproductively, they could lead to losses of businesses and other properties, bankruptcies known in the local discourses as *kissara*, as opposed to *tirfe* or profits and prosperity. 'It is how wisely and productively one can use *equbs* [and other resources] that matters rather than how much one can access,' said Sirgaga, a key respondent from the Silte group who also led *equbs* for a long time (interview, Addis Ababa, April 12, 2003).

Equbs as Forms of Entrepreneurial Calvinism

Equbs are among the main sources for the economic ethic of the Gurage and new spirit or culture of capitalism in Ethiopia. The *equbs* signify some of the major ways in which Gurage entrepreneurialism represented grassroots civic organizations that emerged from and depended on individual and collective initiatives and activities. *Equbs* provide the fora for the formation and transformation, communication, mediation, and transmission of entrepreneurial ideologies and cultures among members of urban and rural Gurage communities and other Ethiopians.

Each *equb* had its own leaders who mobilized, recruited, educated, and led the members. The leaders and other successful entrepreneurs served as models for and guided and taught others through their behavior, stories, and example. Such exemplary Gurage *equb* leaders included Nega Bonger[14] and Kibru Melese,[15] who are renowned for helping many entrepreneurs succeed. "I participate in several equbs. I have equb at Nega's, Kibru's, Berta's and others [referring to *equb* leaders]. I have a good name and they all respect me. Whenever I ask them to take *equb* at the beginning, they always give me priorities through purchase of the turns. That is how I succeeded," said Zeni, a female entrepreneur (interview, Addis Ababa, March 13, 2004).

The *equb* leaders perform their duties and interact with their members in stunningly evangelical manners, manifesting the social movement dimensions of Gurage entrepreneurialism. One can find parallels between Gurage entrepreneurialism and the Reformation movement, as described by Weber (1992). The Reformation movement leaders, Luther and Calvin, played crucial roles in the development of the new spirit of European capitalism. Similarly, Gurage *equb* leaders such as Nega Bonger and Kibru Melese—the entrepreneurial Calvin and Luther of Ethiopia—contributed tremendously to the rise of new Gurage-turned-Ethiopian entrepreneurial cultures. *Equbs'* roles as social disciplinary fora were crucial in that people join the organizations seeking capital, power, guidance, a sense of calling, and sociocultural nourishment. In many of the stories I collected, *equbs* are framed as liberating organizations that are committed to social and economic work, especially helping startup entrepreneurs.

---

13   Other writers (Hefner 1998, Gupta 1994) also disproved this assertion by Weber.

14   Nega was one of the most successful Gurage entrepreneurs from Ezha, pioneering in hotel industry and diversifying his businesses into large import and export trades and real estate businesses. He was also one of the architects and leaders of Gurage *equbs*, who helped many Gurage entrepreneurs succeed. He passed away in August 2021.

15   Kibru is a very successful businessman from Muher, operating souvenir businesses, large import trade, wholesaling, distributing textile businesses. He is one of the most famous and successful Gurage *equb* leaders.

In Gurage *equb* practices, the leaders and the followers have strong beliefs in the importance of *equbs* to the experience of Gurage and other Ethiopian people's conversion to entrepreneurialism. This self-transforming and liberating process is conceived by many Gurage and other Ethiopians as a Gurage mode of being in the modern Ethiopian world. This process signifies how Gurage entrepreneurial ideology translates into a national Ethiopian entrepreneurial ideology, a mode of constructing national entrepreneurial subjects. Like traditions of migration, *equbs* are crucial ways of recruiting the next generations of non-entrepreneur Gurage and non-Gurage Ethiopians into entrepreneurialism, which came to be translated as Gurageness in the Ethiopian context.

The entrepreneurial stories reveal that elements of Gurage ethnicity and kinship (such as *equb* and *fano* living) were used to develop cooperative ties in the evolution of Gurage entrepreneurialism. However, these positive and inclusive stories that say, 'We were helped by and helped our kin,' reveal only part of the story of Gurage entrepreneurialism. In contrast, there are narratives that revealed that ethnic and kin ties have been manipulated and exploited by some successful entrepreneurs, providing insights into the realities that not all co-ethnics and kin members were welcomed by their coethnic and kin successful entrepreneurs. The stories provided useful insights into how kinship ideology allowed some successful entrepreneurs to access and exploit their kin's unwaged labor. It also provides insights into kinship manipulation and exploitation as an important explanation for some individuals' entrepreneurial success. Sondra Hale also reported that the upper class Nubians manipulated their brethrens for their personal ends (1979). These insights challenge some of the ethnic theories of entrepreneurial success where family and ethnic ties are seen to be based on reciprocal support system, obscuring the existence of the uneven power relations and access to cultural resources.

Conclusion

Studies of ethnic entrepreneurship often discuss migrant group living and rotating savings and credit associations (ROSCAs) for their roles in enabling migrants to generate the capital needed to develop business enterprises. The Gurage data presented here on *fano* living and *equb*s expands our understanding of group living and ROSCAs by describing how they serve as major breeding grounds and tools for spreading Gurage entrepreneurial ideologies. By living in *fano* houses, young Gurage immigrants are enculturated/socialized into new ways of being Gurage by the inspiring stories they hear every night from elder (and kin) migrants. These stories constitute a central way for being and becoming entrepreneurial. *Fano* living, in addition, fosters collaboration at work based on kin ties which help Gurage adjust to new cultural situations/contexts.

In a similar way, *equbs* facilitate generations of Gurage migrants being socialized into entrepreneurship. In my interviews with three generations of Gurage entrepreneurs, *equbs* are the most cited source for generating entrepreneurial capital. In this sense, they embody the organizational structure and ideology of Gurage entrepreneurialism. As with *fano* living, weekly *equb* meetings present stories of entrepreneurial success that, in repeatedly being shared among members, reinforce a Gurage ethic of capitalism. As the Gurage state, "*equb* makes man (people]."

The above account illuminates ways in which Gurage emerged as successful entrepreneurs from marginalized serfs to managers of their own businesses during the 1940s, to the 1970s, focusing particularly on the role played by *fano* group living and *equb*s. The Gurage creative use of what I term a three-legged entrepreneurial scaffolding—personal characteristics, ethnic-cultural resources (especially in the form of *fano*-group living and *equb*s) and state support—produced a Gurage national entrepreneurial class, that replaced the expatriate business groups that dominated Ethiopia's commerce for decades and which, critically, helped create the modern Ethiopian capitalist economy. In the process, it fostered a new, Gurage cultural identity as entrepreneurs.

CHAPTER 2

Of Sciences and Startups: An Anthropological Perspective on Academic Venturing

LORA KOYCHEVA

Introduction

It is not uncommon for her to be rejected, but she perseveres, and today is yet another trial of her persuasion skills. Pacing back and forth in front of the jury—two men and a woman, all in dark suits—with a gamely smile on her face, she notes that the technology she has come to pitch will make history possible. She pulls up her visuals and explains it. "That´s great," says one of the men, "but what you have told us today sounds less like science, and more like science fiction." In many ways, this is a last drop. She fairly explodes, "All I´m asking is for you to have the tiniest bit of vision, to just step back for one minute to look at the big picture. To take chance on something, this might be the most profoundly impactful moment for humanity..." Disgruntled, she admits in the end that today is the last chance for her to raise funds for her vision, and that she has failed now at doing so for 13 months.

Entrepreneurship research has examined this phenomenon of perseverance in one´s vision and goal toward introducing novelty in society from a variety of perspectives, offering a number of constructs to conceptualize it, measure it, and theorize it. From entrepreneurial passion, as the "intense positive feelings experienced by engagement in entrepreneurial activities" (Cardon et al. 2009: 517), to entrepreneurial self-efficacy as the "the degree to which individuals believe they are capable of performing the tasks associated with new-venture management" (Forbes 2005: 599), to studying in an extraordinary detail the various psychological forces behind entrepreneurial motivations and intentions as "the conscious state of mind that precedes action and directs attention toward entrepreneurial behaviors such as starting a new business and becoming an entrepreneur" (Moriano et al. 2012:165). In sum, who is an entrepreneur and why have been pivotal questions in the field of entrepreneurship studies for some nearly three decades now (Gartner 1989).

The woman in my vignette is not an entrepreneur, however. Quite to the contrary, she is a researcher. I purposefully mislead my reader here, in making use of a well-known scene from the movie *Contact* (1997), in which Jodie Foster´s character must find a wealthy backer for her ambitious research in the pursuing of making contact with an extraterrestrial sentient species. I do so in order to use it as an opening gambit to challenge the readers to examine how popular discourses about what it takes to be and behave like an entrepreneur have taken hold in our collective imagination and to drive home the point that a paradox simmers below the perceptible surface of academic entrepreneurship—the phenomenon which I have been studying for two years and which is at the heart of this paper. This paradox is that, ostensibly, both researchers and entrepreneurs are people with vision, deeply motivated to pursue their goal, and requiring high degrees of resilience to overcome the significant challenges of bringing something new into the world, whether challenging an incumbent theory or an incumbent business. Both operate in highly competitive and goal-oriented settings. Both have to pitch for money. It should follow that they share the same mindset. Yet most academics will never go on to found a business. Why?

The question is of significant economic, as well as intellectual, importance. Well-developed entrepreneurial activity contributes to overall societal wealth (Van Stel, Caree, and Thurik 2005) and is also a good driver for regional development and prosperity (Hayter 1997; Bramwell and Wolfe 2008; Guerrero et al 2018; Niosi 2006). The promotion and support of entrepreneurial activities therefore is often of key interest for economic development policy for a variety of stakeholders, from international to national to local government agents. One such area of development has been academic entrepreneurship: the creation of research spin-off companies by university faculty (Shane 2004) and more recently also by various other agents in the academy, such as students and post-docs (e.g. Hayter et al. 2017). Starting in the United States in the early 1980s with the passing of the Bayh-Dole Act (Aldridge and Audretsch 2011), enabling the commercialization efforts in academia, largely for the life sciences (Grimaldi et al. 2011), and adopted more recently as a model for academic operations in Europe, university-based entrepreneurship is today a domain of significant activity and financial potential, giving rise to "entrepreneurial universities" (Etzkovitz 1993). How to create and stimulate startup culture in the academic context, therefore, remains a question of continued relevance and interest, for both developed and developing countries. Its multifaceted answers have implications not only for the creation of novel approaches to entrepreneurship training and development, but more broadly, for the potential of spinning off companies rooted in scientific research which, if only incentivized and enabled in the appropriate way, can contribute additionally to such economic development.

Entrepreneurship research has dealt with this question from multiple angles, which I will briefly review in what follows – from a focus on policy to examining institutional climate; from personal traits to identities – yet almost overwhelmingly through a psychological lens and explanatory frameworks. That is, regardless of which construct is being studied, the focus has been always on the individual level, rather than to pay attention on how such level is implicated in, constructed by, acted on and in turn constitutive of organizational arrangements, discourses and practices: in other words, entrepreneurial culture. In this paper, I offer a remedial contribution to this status quo in entrepreneurship research and suggest that opening up a space for anthropological analysis offers a variety of new analytical vocabularies and theoretical angles through which to theorize and understand entrepreneurship. I examine questions of anthropological relevance in the entrepreneurship domain with a focus on academic entrepreneurship specifically to offer a more holistic understanding of university-based entrepreneurship. I draw on my more than 24-month-long ethnographic work in an academic ecosystem in

Western Europe and on insights produced by two distinct studies. One is an ethnography of a startup developing cutting edge engineering research and another of a "makeathon," geared toward the creation of regular ventures at the masters' degree level. I examine the various discourses circulating in both the academic and the startup sphere; how they converged and diverged in the academic ecosystem, and how they created a shifting ground in the ecosystem – one difficult for its members to navigate due to the oft-divergent logics and demands of both cultures which had direct impact on the way they considered venturing. Specifically, I demonstrate that within a single institutional context, that of the university, there were two concurrent ludic cultures – that of play and that of games – and they often conflicted with one another. I discuss how an anthropological approach to understanding university-based venturing offers an insight into yet another dimension of the phenomenon, in ways which dominant psychological approaches do not. In so doing, the purposes of the paper are multifold.

I conclude that a complication of the concept of the "mindset" as currently prominent in entrepreneurship with one grounded in the psychological anthropological posits that the mindset exists always *in* culture will be a fruitful way forward. I explore how this creates a zone of better rapprochement between entrepreneurship and anthropology as disciplines studying venturing. Also, I offer an example of how a traditional ethnographic inquiry in the otherwise difficult to study ethnographically new venture creation context can unfold. On a more practical note, the paper makes suggestions on how anthropology can lend its considerable methodological repertoire to the study and the building of startup cultures and ecosystems; and what the challenges are for anthropology in so doing.

A Tale of Two Studies: An Ethnography of University Venturing

Both the makeathons and the moonshot venture—the two studies upon which I draw in this paper—are underrepresented in the entrepreneurship literature for several reasons. Although anthropological accounts of hackathons have been proffered to study the moral and political imagination of the neoliberal present (e.g., Coleman and Golub 2008), makeathons (time-pressured formats of making, doing, and hacking together with others notably producing mechanical prototypes rather than digital products) are still understudied in both anthropology and entrepreneurship. They have garnered the interest of entrepreneurship researchers as sites and context of venturing only recently because they are an emergent phenomenon, arising out of the maker movements and the constructions of makerspaces—communal structures, often with gym-like business models of paying a membership fee to have access to state-of-the-art technology—in the late 2000s (van Holm 2015; Bowder, Aldridge and Bradley 2019). In turn, moonshot venturing, developing innovation whose adoption is at least a decade away, constitutes a kind of innovation and venturing rarely undertaken outside of government or corporate labs. Although moonshot venturing is heavily dependent on research, few university ecosystems actually promote such kind of ventures because the nature of the innovation introduces a new product in a new market— in the"suicide quadrant" of innovation (Sarasvathy 2009)— remains very difficult to build, test, and deploy in real-life contexts, thus making it impossible for fast commercialization. This is because venture capital typically stays away from funding such endeavors; returns will be not quick enough, whereas grants and other public funds are often neither plentiful enough nor fast enough to fund the necessary innovation. It is not a coincidence that most known examples of moonshot venturing are embedded either within government structures, such as DARPA in the United States, or within large corporations, such as Google´s X Moonshot Factory (x.company) and Waymo (www.waymo.com)

Since both the makeathons and the moonshot were developed and run by students, most of them doctoral students, in collaboration with various departments and postdocs at the university made them excellent sites for studying university venturing also especially because starting up by students, rather than tenured and established faculty, remains understudied in the entrepreneurship literature. I would like to say that this gap in the literature was what I was pursuing, but, in a time-honored ethnographic fashion, I followed my "ethnographic hunch" (Pink 2021) to what looked interesting. In this case, it was a bright pink poster advertising the kickoff of the next edition of the makeathons two weeks hence, on my first day of arriving in the ecosystem.

Just Push Play: Makeathons and the Culture of the Playful

Makeathons are difficult to study qualitatively. They are very busy events, with a lot happening nonstop and with multiple teams involved in active creative work. They are also highly dissipative, with small group gatherings forming ad hoc and disbanding quickly after they are over, all of which does not lend itself to the highly controlled approach in the Eisenhardt and Gioia methods, prominent in qualitative entrepreneurship research (Eisenhardt 1989; Gehman et al. 2018). Ethnography, in its improvisational nature and go-with-the-flow approach to messy realities, was an apt methodology.

I collaborated with the makeathons leaders—"the orga crew" —between March 2018 and April 2019, following them and the masters' students who participated in the lab course, for which they also got credit, through their entrepreneurial journeys for four iterations of the format. The format itself was always 14 days, including the two weekends in between. Students from various faculties, mostly from the engineering and life sciences, would apply in advance in a highly competitive selection process since the course was one of the most popular on campus. Students would go from being individuals who have never met to full-fledged startup teams, with a (preferably) working prototype, a validated business plan, and an investor-ready pitch in only two weeks, going through what Liffshitz-Assaf et al. (2018) have theorized as a temporal manipulation in breaking and compressing time. In March 2018, as a preliminary study, I was mostly observing and getting familiar with the format, the activities it promoted, and the specifics of business and engineering: such as low-fidelity prototype, lean canvass, and Raspberry Pi–the exotics of innovation. Because I am also trained in linguistic anthropology and interfered somewhat vociferously with their pitch training on the day before demo day in pointing out a number of things they could improve in their demo preps form a linguistic perspective, after some discussion with one of the founders of the format, I ended up embedded in the makeathons as a coach for pitch training and product validation. This enabled a specific vantage point and role in the context which would otherwise be very difficult to obtain in the entrepreneurship context (Briody and Stewart 2019). Additionally, I also invited all participant of each "batch" of the makeathons to an interview reflecting on their experience in search of an answer to questions of how these students develop ideas about their own self-development as (potential) entrepreneurs. Over the course of the year with the makeathons, I interviewed 57 students, complementing my ethnographic notes of the realities of the makeathon.

These realities were appropriately chaotic, for a process notorious for its uncertainty. Piles of Post-It notes covering wall to wall; Nerf guns for end of day fights when people needed a boost or a creative way to release tensions in the teams; the smell of burnt plywood of prototypes mixing in the air with the whiff of melted cheese sandwiches that the teams would down in a hurry with bitter coffee made in a grubby industrial coffee machine in constant need of rerunning: this is how a typical day of the makeathon would feel like. Many of the participants would sleep there: some bringing camping gear, some improvising beds out of whatever soft surface they would find lying around the building. Rarely anyone would have time to go home to shower or run some personal errand in between a steady downpour of tasks in need of completion against the clock. This included most of the coaches, who were fielding a range of issues every team had: from team conflict and people crying (with people instructed to come to me if this were to happen), to prototypes failing, to being unable to convince their first customer to sign a letter of intent. At any point in time, every single coach was being hailed, in one corner of the open makeathon space or another. It´s the typical environment of an innovation makeathons—a space of extreme devotion and extreme mess.

"FAKE IT TILL YOU MAAAAAKE IIIIIIT!!!!!" One would hear often in the distance coaches bellowing in an effort of animating teams whose prototype had just flopped, effectively preventing them to "demo or die" during demo day.

"Fake it until you make it." "Fail fast and often." "Better ask for forgiveness than for permission:" minimum basics, such as agile prototyping methods, lean canvass and SCRUM, aside, these were the three essential de-facto lessons which the makeathon was trying to instill in the would-be entrepreneurs. It is, as reminded again and again by the coaches, the bread and butter of innovation and venturing, and the three dispositions no entrepreneur can do without. These are, as participants would later tell me in their individual interviews, the three single-most valuable lessons they have learned for business and life, not only in the makeathons but also, for many interviewees, at university as a whole; lessons that their own departments have not taught them. Faking, failing, and breaking the rules—this is what it takes to be an entrepreneur in the ethos which the program was instilling in its students.

Faking (in the sense of mimicking), failing (in the sense of coming short of established norms and expectations), and breaking rules (whether willingly or because they are oblivious to them) is something that children do in exploring the world around them and devising their own improvisational, creative, and ultimately, playful ways of forging their identities and testing their place in the world (e.g., Sicart 2014). Management literature has long recognized the creative underpinnings of innovation (e.g., Amabile and Pratt 2016), and in fact, many of my interviewees note that "fun"—despite the intensity, stress, and high-pressure environment of the makeathons—was what they experienced and loved most about the format. What is more the makeathons have given them the ability to position themselves in the shoes of entrepreneurs, in however time-compressed a format, by going through the steps of nascent venturing. This "as-if" process (Koycheva 2019) has given them the ability to reflect upon their own abilities, ambitions, and plans as potential entrepreneurs.

Thus, one participant noted that taking part in the makeathons was "an intense experience…I knew when I got to [the makeathon] that it was going to be an experiment for me as well. So when I got there, I had very high expectations because I wanted to participate in [the makeathon] since my late Bachelors…[and]…how to say what the experience was…[an experiment] because there are some ways in the ways I interact with people and I wanted to know if they are still there and be aware of them as they occur, like when we worked as a team […] and that was something that I wanted to try in a safe environment" Another participant said, "[the makeathon] crazy, […] as cool as I thought it would be because I didn't necessarily do it for the credits because I could've taken any other course but I heard from so many people that this is a really cool thing to do, so that´s why I did it, I didn't necessarily do it for the grades or the credits, I did it more for the fun and to experience it." Yet another suggested that "It was very creative and also a bit of pressure, but also I have learned very much and […] it was one of the first times I could apply the stuff I learned." And another synthesized well a sentiment well prominent in many interview as to why such a format is a good idea in the engineering curriculum: "[the makeathon] was a very interesting experience for me because so far, I´ve worked on, let´s say very specialized projects […] and this was very different because I usually worked with engineers, this was all over and it was much more about quickly getting to do things whereas in classical engineering you think and you slowly…it takes months getting anywhere. A very different experience. Very fun. […] It felt much more active, it felt you had to rely more on your gut feeling as opposed to trying to analyze all the situations. I really liked working with people from different backgrounds because it made me realize certain things, such as how you go about a task, depends on what your background is, and who claims responsibilities, and how you kind of bounce back from each other, like a team dynamics, which was a steep learning curve."

This culture of "fun" and "play," of open, unstructured, improvisational, and messy experimentation within a safe space is, as it turned out, at the heart of a tension that would soon emerge as a recurrent preoccupation in terms of organizing the makeathon and searching for new ways to enable the actual creation of startups. At a retrospective meeting the orga team held in May 2018 after the iteration I observed, there was quite a bit of soul-searching how the makeathons would proceed in future, since most of the current leaders were leaving (some were completing their PhDs and postodcs, some wanted to focus on their own ventures) and new leaders were entering. One key question of contention was whether the "playground" feel of the format was to be kept or discarded for a more mature, more methodological way of approaching innovation. "Just for fun" was what one of the postdocs associated with the makeathons was very vocally and passionately insisting upon, arguing for keeping the ethos of play in the format, while another one of the founding members, a doctoral student, explained later to me that they always envisioned the program as "a kind of a sandbox" where experimentation in form, essence, and operations could be carried out (much like in programming) without the risk of a real damage in real life settings.

Such a culture of play is highly consistent with and conductive of the effectual logic of entrepreneurship (Sarasvathy 2009) as the highly non-linear, contextual, and situational and processes of entrepreneurial bricolage (Baker and Nelson 2005), entrepreneurship research´s key explanatory frameworks on how venturers make do in the recombinant and creative use of resources in the pursuit of their venture ideas. Yet play, as a practice deeply universal to human ability to make sense of the world and to experience new roles and social positions before adopting them fully, is not an analytical framework through which entrepreneurship research theorizes the startup phenomenon.

A Very Serious Game: Moonshots between the World of Research and Business

"I don't know what you´re doing," a doctoral student in engineering and a team member of the moonshot told me angrily in the cold January midafternoon, as we took a walk to clear our heads before continuing work on a last minute piece of scholarly writing we were working on together. As with most things in our overcrowded schedules, this had been left to be executed in the last moment. "We keep hacking things, but this stuff can´t be faked. It´ll be shoddy. And it can't hurt me, but it´ll be bad for you, cuz you are a researcher."

The words startle me, because, caught up in the "fail fast and often" ethos of startup world, not only in the makeathon context, but also here, in the moonshot team, with whom I had been collaborating for almost two years by then, I forget that acting out of a space of experimentation is not always well regarded in academia, and certainly not all failures are alike without consequences, and only full of learning potential and no danger. When I went back to my desk and reconsidered her remark at length, I ended up getting cold feet for fear the writing is not perfect enough and too shoddy (forgetting all that the makeathon taught about being proud of one's prototypes) and I pulled out of the whole endeavor, because, sure enough, I had been reminded that in the academic context, failure is not fun learning. Failure is failure.

Being a researcher illuminated the tensions and conflicted attitudes that various team members had to entrepreneurship and academia as career choices because I became a figure upon whom the team members projected their own understandings of what "being a researcher" meant and involved. For some, it helped initially, in various ways, to accept me, since quite a few of the team were doctoral students, some were postdoctoral, and a few had doctoral ambitions of their own. "Anything for science," was the slightly uncomfortable answer of one team member when I was first going through the informed consent procedure with them. But being a researcher also was detrimental in many ways: some other members were resistant to me becoming more involved with the team by way of my increasing interactions because I was perceived as "not a professional," and yet others, who needed a long while to accept me, because they saw the world of academia as completely devoid of value.

The venture CEO always took it upon himself to teach me "venturing" but often got exasperated because, as he signaled on multiple occasions over the years I would "think like a researcher" and have a "researcher mindset." When pressed what that means, he noted once that "researchers always analyze very deeply before they act, to a level that's not practical in business." On the other hand, the postdocs saw me as an ally of sorts, or at least an understanding shoulder to cry on when research at the venture "was not done properly" as one of them said, because "they [the company] keep hacking stuff… it needs to be reproducible for it to have scientific value."

The world of moonshot venturing creates the kind of innovation that is at least a few decades away from being widely adopted. A such, it requires not only a steady scientific research program but also an even steadier stream of preferably fast funds. It is, therefore, uneasily straddling both the world of academia and the world of business, and, if undertaken privately, it must respond to both. This tension between venture world, with its fast-paced logic, accelerated and shortened timelines that demanded agility and willingness to go out of one's comfort zone in pursuit of an opportunity, and above all to be able to act on opportunities quickly, and the world of research where demands placed on individual members of the team from their respective departments, with a focus on "reproducibility," grant writing, publishing, and general best practice kept coming up also as tensions in meetings about decision-making, and resulted in several exits from the team in the long run by those who identified more as researchers and less like engineers who start up a venture.

This is not to say that they did so lightly or easily, and that being part of the startup did not create doubts in their own professional self-understanding about who they were and what they were doing. "Lora, why are we researchers?" fairly exploded in a loud voice one late night one of the team members, as we were sitting in an empty subway car on our return commute home. "Why am I doing this stuff and getting paid so little, when I can be working fully commercial and putting down on a mortgage for a house?" Working for a well-known local research laboratory would create more security but would be "less fun; they are all depressed as f*** there, just doing research, they have a soulless look about them," my friend continued musing out loud. We reflected a bit on "what's in it for us in research, really," and how far away both our imaginary mortgages were.

It was one of the last times when we entertained such perceivable freedom away from the academy´s strictures together. Pressured to publish or perish and get grants or lose our positions at our respective departments, we had little time to socialize or work together further.

Academics, Entrepreneurs, and Academic Entrepreneurship between Play and Games: Disciplinary Variations on a Theme

Founding from within the academy has been intensively interrogated, from a variety of angles. A lot is now known of the phenomenon since it came on the scholarly radar as a topic of research in the 1980s – so much so that there are specialized journals, such as *The Journal of Technology Transfer and Research Policy.* Since their potential for commercializing research has been greater than that of the social sciences and the humanities, life sciences and medical sciences units within universities have been frequently examined (e.g., Colyvas 2007; Haessleur and Colyvas 2011). The emergence of science parks and technology transfer offices and their effect on starting up from within the academy have been studied in a variety of contributions (Huygh et al. 2016; Rothaermel and Thursby 2005; Clarysse et al 2007). A lot of the attention has been paid on regional variation and geographic clustering of innovation, as the commercialization of science began becoming more prominent (Fini et al 2011; Etzkovitz and Klofsten 2005). Issues of policy and strategic challenges, , have also been examined (e.g. Siegel and Wright 2015).

It is only more recently that the entrepreneurship research has moved away from this macro perspective and started paying attention to human factors. Almost inevitably so, however, research has been animated by psychological approaches, concerned with individuals and their attributions (e.g., Hmieleski and Powell 2018) and what their mindsets and thinking are. This is so because the overwhelming consensus in the entrepreneurship literature suggests that entrepreneurs are unique in their thinking, and decades of research, too prolix to summarize here, have attempted to "open the black box" of entrepreneurs´ minds (Breugst and Preller 2020) in an attempt to answer the elusive questions of "how entrepreneurs think" and "who is an entrepreneur" (see Shepherd and Patzelt 2018 for a comprehensive review on entrepreneurial cognition). This is because the entrepreneur, whether alone or in a team, is the key driving figure behind novel business creation.

However, these approaches are usually influenced by one of entrepreneurship's founding discipline—psychology—and as a result, this has heavily tipped the scholarly conversation toward discussing the "entrepreneurial mindset," spelling out the aggregate picture of types of individuals, and individual minds. Rarely are the questions asked and examined through an anthropological lens, which provides a much-needed additional dimension, examining and theorizing entrepreneurship as a lived reality enmeshed with a variety of mutually constitutive, often contradictory, and always dynamic practices, meanings, and actors within the space of any given context. Moreover, such psychological research largely either subsumes culture under mindset or ignores the cultural dimensions of academic entrepreneurship altogether.

And even when aspects of academic entrepreneurship that could potentially be construed as remedial in this otherwise swing between macro/micro extremes, as has been the case with "entrepreneurial climate," researchers have conceptualized it in terms of psychological perception, rather than in terms of intricate interplay between norms and meaning, as an anthropological approach would (for climate, see Geissler et al. 2010). In fact, the tenet of thinking and theorizing in "mindsets" is so strong in entrepreneurship, that obtaining it has been suggested not only for individuals, but also for entire organizations, in a telling but disturbing subsuming of what could be construed as "culture" under the construct of "mindset" (e.g. Klofsten et al. 2019). In such a scenario, the onus to become entrepreneurial is exclusively on the individual, who should change their mindset. That the mind exists in culture, and is accordingly shaped by it (e.g., Hollan 2005; Levy and Hollan 1998) is hardly ever a dynamic that entrepreneurship considers empirically, theorizes, or else suggests as practical advice.

For most anthropologists, this would not come as a surprise, given our discipline's long-standing tense and often awkward engagement with psychology's epistemological framework and methodological approaches in both scholarly conversations (e.g., Fish 2000, Greenfield 2000, Hickman 2010) and the applied milieu of business anthropology (e.g., Sunderland and Denny 2003, 190-191; Morais and de Waal Malefyt 2010, 46). In addition, anthropology has tended to see entrepreneurship as a field of practice differently, and largely as part and parcel of the purview of economic anthropology. For example, Bernard Wong (1998) has provided a compelling picture on the entrepreneurship strategies of Chinese immigrants in the Bay Area, and Hannah Marshall has looked at how entrepreneurship programs for ex-convicts in Uganda provide a way back into society (2018*).*

Other social science fields, on the other hand, have viewed these developments of com-mercialization stemming from the university in a very different vein, usually carrying political critique, and have theorized it peripherally, as part and parcel of larger shifts in the life of the academy in the past three decades which have heralded not only regimes of neoliberal audit and governance. Academia, as Pierre Bourdieu has powerfully demonstrated, is an institu-tion with highly stratified and codified practices, aimed at maintaining not only the rigidly hierarchical structures of the academy, but also to promote and reproduce the academic's habitus (Bourdieu 1988). For Germany, where my two studies were conducted, this is perhaps even more so, as recent work has suggested that German academic life is even more rigid in its hierarchies than other countries – for example see Vita Peacock's discussion of hierarchy in the Max Planck System (2016) as stemming from older models of the German monarchy. Although venturing from within the Max Planck Society has been studied, even then, spinning off is a tied to personal networks (e.g., Kraebel and Muller 2009). Although scientists have been shown to be innovative and risk-taking in their work (Foster et al. 2015), academia remains a world of metrics, cultures of "excellence" embodied in citations and grants; in other words, a world of rules, of a game to be played and won. To fail fast and often, to ask for forgiveness and not for permission, and to fake it until you make it are rallying cries that only spell out trouble in the world of academia.

So where psychology-influenced colleagues see individuals with specific traits and cog-nitive abilities, in my research I also see that those considering venturing in the academic context were also enmeshed in two very different cultures: one (that of academia) a culture of rule following and one (that of entrepreneurship) of rule breaking and unstructured experi-mentation, each with distinct temporal dimensions, practice logics, and discourses all acting on these individuals who must then in turn act back on their environment. This was clearly visible in the stark difference between how doctoral and postdoctoral researchers from the moonshot differed in their self-conceptualization as being also entrepreneurs vis à vis the ease with which masters students from the makeathon would discuss themselves as entrepreneurs. The majority of the makeathon participants, for example, when asked to reflect on who they were as individuals, would often discuss their identities as specialists who are experimenting in interdisciplinary settings and beginning to see themselves like entrepreneurs, but would also discuss their identity experiences in terms evocative of play, playfulness, and playing. They would also have less of a tension with ideas of entrepreneurship than my interlocutors from the moonshot, who, at a more advanced educational level and at a much farther profession-alization stage, were struggling with the counter-logics of entrepreneurship, with its call for disruption, and academia, with its demands for discipline. Masters students had an easier time imagining and experiencing themselves as entrepreneurs because they had spent less time in the disciplinarian halls of the doctoral and postdoctoral circuit. Simply put, they lacked the academic habitus, which made their becoming of entrepreneurs easier.

Finally, these identity struggles also happen against a broader cultural ideational backdrop that mythologizes dropping out of college. Although Google was found by two doctoral students, the overwhelmingly popular mythology of the startup world supports an anti-academic ideology. Dropping out of university to found multi-billion-dollar businesses, as in the case of Steve Jobs and Mark Zuckerberg, creates a glorified if not necessarily realistic picture of the relationship between founding and the academy. Such a backdrop further created pressures for some interlocutors, and was variously embedded, reconfigured but almost never challenged, in their understandings of what it means to be an entrepreneur.

Challenges and Opportunities for Anthropology in and of Entrepreneurship: Concluding Remarks

What are the challenges for anthropology, then, in and of entrepreneurship, and how can the two fields start developing a common ground for a rapprochement, which is, despite its exciting potential, still difficult and largely missing (Briody and Steward 2019)? And how can an anthropologically informed approach contribute to the economically important question about promoting more startup creation from within the university, whether at master, doctoral or postdoctoral, or scientist levels?

Purely psychological and economic approaches understandably miss key dimensions of a complex picture. Our discipline´s distinctive contributions remain largely epistemological and methodological, which is well known. Anthropology has well-rehearsed debates about its very "kinky empiricism" (Rutherford 2012), and its unique way of studying phenomena first and foremost by paying attention to mutually constitutive practices and in relational terms above all. Questions of philosophical import, such as generalizability and hypothesizing (see Fish 2000; Greenfield 2000 for psychology and anthropology specifically, and Wolcott 2005: 147 -211 for a general discussion) are good to keep in mind, yet they rarely lead to practi-cal resolutions. In this paper, in offering an ethnography of academic entrepreneurs, I have started to demonstrate how an attention to practices, discourses, and even temporalities and materialities can complement the dominant in entrepreneurship paradigm of "mindset" and start thinking instead about how the mindset exists in—and is shaped by—specific cultures. This helps provide a more nuanced, more granular understanding of the "mindset," and one that locates the inquiry and the theoretical modeling of the entrepreneurship as a nested, inter-level phenomenon (what the anthropological lingo refers to as "mutually constitutive") between an individual, a team, and an organization, rather than as a phenomenon understood in terms of linear and mutually disconnected levels.

Ostensibly the very similar mindsets (resilient, visionary, persistent) and even often similar practices (pitching for money, iterating on the original idea) result in very different outcomes between those who become entrepreneurs and those who do not in academia. This strongly suggests that it is not so much individual psychological processes, rather that the structures in which they occur to which we need to be paying attention. This does not require us to be dismissive of psychological processes, but rather conceptualizes them differently as part and parcel of larger structures, discourses, and systems of meaning and action that shape them and are in turn shaped by the mind. Thus, anthropology can lend its considerable methodological strengths and repertoire in capturing otherwise elusive aspects of lived culture to the academic venturing sector in many ways.

Anthropology can continue to challenge existing explanatory models in entrepreneurship which start with assumption and do research by "gap filling" while missing out on important questions and dynamics that should be asked "from below"—those rooted in what the entrepreneurs do. There, the challenge remains largely how to translate anthropology. We would need to translate it to our colleagues from entrepreneurship research. The danger there is how to address long standing epistemological, methodological, and even conceptual differences without stalling the conversation there, but rather using it as a springboard to novel integrations. We need to translate it to entrepreneurs, for whom anthropology as a source of insights and help is virtually unknown. And we need to translate it to some of our own colleagues within anthropology. Rather than remaining purely in the domain of being a "theory of description" (Nader 2011), how do we make anthropology and ethnography "a theory of intervention"? At a practical level, there are key reorientations to which the discipline will likely have to agree, not only in the applied vein in which we have excellent examples already in the domain of business anthropology, where anthropologists are consultants, but also what it means for the role of the discipline in the world.

Such a reorientation can be seen also in a positive light. Anthropology can continue to reinvent itself in adapting its hallmark political dispositions and methodological strengths toward new horizons of action and application, retaining and even increasing its relevance to domains hitherto unfamiliar with the discipline's value for them. And that can only be, in all the best ways, entrepreneurial.

Acknowledgments: I would like to gratefully acknowledge the generous support of the Joachim Herz Foundation (Germany) in conducting this research. The research would not have been possible by the extreme generosity of time, attention, and sharing work and dreams with me by a long list of collaborators—now friends—who participated in the research. I cannot name your names, but you know who you are. I hope we will all be unicorns one day. All errors and mistakes, as always, my own, and the views and opinions expressed here are mine alone and do not represent anyone else associated with the studies or this text.

CHAPTER 3

Entrepreneurship in the "New Normal": Pandemic Ruptures and Continuities among Agra's Tourism Entrepreneurs

RIDDHI BHANDARI, O.P. Jindal Global University, India

Introduction: *"This [phone number] is currently out of order"*

It started with phone calls–sometime around August 2020, I noticed that many of my research participants–tour guides, shop owners, photographers and small boutique hotel owners–were increasingly unreachable on their phones. This was odd because, for Agra's tourism entrepreneurs, digital connectivity was critical to their entrepreneurialism: to be readily available for tourists as well as connected with other entrepreneurs with whom they worked in partnership, to share information on tourists and their itinerary. However, starting in mid–2020, I would call different entrepreneurs and find automated messages, like, "due to the inability to recharge the phone, this number is currently out of order," switched off or had been disconnected. Sometimes a stranger would answer–they had recently acquired this number and usually did not know the person I had called for. When I inquired about it, entrepreneurs' responses ranged from having damaged their devices and not having stepped out to repair or recharge it, to not needing individual phone numbers anymore because work was slow, and everyone was home bound anyway. Over a period, a trend emerged–Agra's tourism entrepreneurs had been hard hit with the pandemic and with an uncertain source of income, many were downsizing. Tourism had been impacted due to travel restrictions and the closure of key heritage monuments, like the Taj Mahal, and as result, entrepreneurs' work and earnings had dwindled to almost nothing. This had been going on since late 2019–tourism was one of the sectors to get early intimations of the looming pandemic–and with no clear end to the crisis in sight, most entrepreneurs were cutting back on their expenses. Phones, a necessity good in normal times, transformed into luxury items and were being budgeted in an annual review of pandemic planning.

I had already been keenly following the impacts of the pandemic on Agra's entrepreneurs and had stayed in regular touch with many of them, exchanging updates on health and trying to gauge their need for assistance and how best to meet it. But the shift in their phone usage marked an important point for me to comprehend the extent of disruptions in economic life wrought by the pandemic, especially for small-scale and usually self-employed entrepreneurs in Agra's tourism.

This paper draws from my ongoing conversations with entrepreneurs since March 2020, to understand how the pandemic impacted tourism-related entrepreneurship, their struggles to manage the disruptions and attempts at restructuring their economic practices with the ongoing pandemic. Furthermore, I highlight entrepreneurs' assessments of the state in both exacerbating and attempting to alleviate these uncertainties, and their hopes for the future. Together, these narratives are an invitation to critically consider the role of the state in creating a structurally supportive business environment that must extend beyond crises even as it is integral to weather them.

COVID–19: Pandemic Ruptures–the first lockdown

Entrepreneurs considered the shifts in their economic activities with the pandemic through the twin and related registers of rupture and continuity. Beginning with rupture, nearly all entrepreneurs I spoke with said that to those working in tourism, the impending COVID–19 crisis and its economic fallout was visible much before it began to garner public and government attention. Entrepreneurs recalled that tourist footfall in the fall and winter months of 2019 (peak tourism season for international tourists visiting Agra) was suspiciously low, and in retrospect, they connected it to the fact that COVID was already circulating in other parts of the world, as a mysterious flu, that nevertheless impeded the travels and tourism plans of international tourists. Akaash, a tour guide and owner of a small start-up tour operations company, recalled speaking with his business partner and friend in January 2020, and noting with concern, the low number of international tourists in Agra: "We wondered if it was pollution and AQI[1] first, but then, I mentioned to him that there was this virus: my girlfriend in Malaysia had told me about it. By then COVID was already making news in that part of the world [southeast Asia]." This trend had worried Akaash because he had started his tour company in 2017, and by 2019, they were finally beginning to find entrepreneurial stability–of reputation, clientele, and monetary turnover. They had established connections with a few travel agencies and begun to have a recognizable digital presence. In 2019, they had hired 5 employees: 1 web designer, 1 office worker to run errands, 2 tour guides and 1 representative who liaised with hotels and showrooms and addressed tourists' complaints. However, by the end of the year, as COVID sped up and spread out, tourism slowed down, and although the Taj Mahal closed on 16th March 2020, foreign tourists, according to Akaash, had already stopped coming by the end of 2019. With the national lockdown imposed on March 22nd, Akaash counted 180 straight days of zero earnings from his tourism business.

Umar, a shop owner with an assortment of tourism paraphernalia–decorative and domestic marble commodities, like photo frames, ash trays, rolling pin and board, pestle-grinder, hats, leather sandals–too recalled the sudden rupture in economic activity with the pandemic. According to him, before the nationwide lockdown, he earned about INR 30,000 (approximately USD 400) a month, and after expenditure on rent, utilities, restocking his shop, and household expenses, he saved up to INR 10,000 (USD 133) a month. With the national lockdown, Umar recalled six months of inactivity, where he and his three brothers sat at home, with no work and earnings. Their household was able to tide over this period by drawing on savings, his mother and sister's earnings through home-based tailoring work, and his father's pension[2]. "*Tangi mehsoos hui lekin guzaara ho gaya*–we felt the need to tighten our expendi-

---

1 Air Quality Index.
2 Umar's father was a government employee who had passed away nearly two decades ago, and Umar's mother received a widow's share of his pension.

ture, but we were able to make do," he concluded. However, he also pointed out that during this period, there was no relief from rent and electricity bill payment for his shop.

This savings-reliant making do was repeated by many entrepreneurs that I spoke with: Akaash too dipped into his savings, which had been planned for business expansion–the partners wanted to purchase "transport" (a mini-bus and two SUV taxi cabs) for their tourism company. But with savings redirected towards daily expenditure, that have currently whittled down to nothing, these business plans were shelved indefinitely. The women in Akaash's family, just like Umar's mother, also emerged as pivotal economic actors that provided some consistency. The earnings from his *bua* (father's sister) and mother's small stationery and daily goods shop had kept money in circulation in their household, relieving Akaash of the possible pressures of being the sole earner with no source of income.

Others, however, were not that fortunate. Many of Agra's tourism entrepreneurs relied on daily earnings and while in peak season, these could be substantial, they did not usually materialize into deep savings. I recall Faisal, a tour guide who worked from the ticket-window outside the west entrance gate of the Taj Mahal, calling me in late November 2020, to say that he was looking for work outside of tourism and if I had any leads, to let him know. He was willing to travel to southern India as well, should work be located there. He was not an outlier in this regard: I heard of many tour guides and photographers who moved out of tourism, and began hawking and vendoring – selling fruits and vegetables on a mobile cart (*thela*)–, masks and hand-sanitizers in makeshift "shops" by the side of main roads and markets, or fried foods and snacks in the evenings in mobile kiosks. This, for Agra's tourism entrepreneurs, was a decidedly downward move in terms of employment and aspirations. During the time of my fieldwork, many entrepreneurs had gravitated towards tourism from exactly these jobs and despite the uncertainty and risks in tourism, saw it as a much more respectable sector of employment than working as mechanics, vendors, and hawkers. For example, in 2017, a tour guide's father had finally shuttered his fried meats stall once his son began to work as a tour guide, and had rented a wall from Umar's shop, from where he sold sunglasses. The father–son duo had explained this move as one towards comfort in old age – the proximity to heat, oil, and exposure to the weather *and* the police was taxing, and they wanted some years of "decent" work for him. In 2020, the father had moved out of Umar's shop and returned to selling fried meats in the evening on a makeshift kiosk. His son had started helping him there.

Ongoing Economic Impacts
The fact that the pandemic may have altered the tourism market in Agra in a lasting way hit entrepreneurs once the national lockdown was lifted, tourism monuments were opened (although still regulated with weekend closures and a cap on the number of tourists permitted inside), and market activities were permitted. Despite the unlocking, tourists did not return and eventually, those that returned were very different from the ones entrepreneurs expected or hoped for.

Altered Tourist Clientele
International flights did not resume, and international tourists have not yet returned to Agra[3]. For entrepreneurs like Akaash, these international tourists comprised core, desirable clientele. Domestic tourists that entrepreneurs like Umar and Faisal depended on for their earnings, were widely

---

3   Commercial international flights scheduled to resume by December 15, 2021, have been further postponed till January 30, 2022, due to the Omicron variant.

perceived to be afraid and unwilling to travel, facing both their own economic uncertainties and pay cuts as well as due to concerns over safety, hygiene, and physical distancing during COVID. Entrepreneurs were also of the opinion that the continued closure of the Taj Mahal during weekends[4], well after the lockdown was lifted, further depressed possibilities of any tourism activity.

A few entrepreneurs also spoke of how the pandemic changed tourism patterns. Agra's tourism economy, where a significant portion of the local population is directly or indirectly engaged, has always desired that tourists stay in Agra for a few days, spending time and money not only on monuments but also food, accommodation, and shopping. However, whistle-stop trips[5], encouraged by the promotion of the "Golden Triangle[6]", aided by good connectivity between Delhi-Agra-Jaipur through rail and road, and facilitated by the absence of an international airport in Agra, have always been a cause for concern for local entrepreneurs, as they facilitated quick entry and exit to and from Agra. With the pandemic, this quick mode of travel seems to have solidified further as tourists' preferred choice of travel. Entrepreneurs believed that with the pandemic, most tourists that were visiting Agra were from within a 250-300 kms distance, which meant that they often came for day trips, usually in their own vehicles, preferred self-reliant visits to the Taj Mahal, unaccompanied by tour guides or photographers, stayed for one meal, and did not spend money purchasing local, familiar goods. This shift in clientele meant that tourists were spending even lesser time and money in Agra, and only on the purchase of tickets and limited food and beverages, leaving shop owners, hoteliers, tour guides and photographers without any predictable earnings.

Second Wave–From Uncertainty to Precarity

Entrepreneurs were also unanimous in their assessment that the second wave (March–June 2021) and the subsequent localized lockdowns, including the closure of the Taj Mahal, had hit them much more severely because business had not picked up, savings were running thin, and aid and assistance from civil society organizations, citizens groups, local leaders and one's kith and kin, had also dried up. Umar recalled this period as one of reckoning with the full extent and anticipated long-term economic impacts of the pandemic. "Up until then, we had reasoned that it's lockdown, no one can move around but once unlocking begins, businesses will start back up, we'll get back on our feet. But when the lockdown was over and we used to open our shops and no one would come, that was very hard. Many days would pass without making any sale. I can't even explain to you the anxiety that I would feel–I didn't feel at peace either at home or in my shop," he said.

Entrepreneurs that had relied on their savings in the hope that the economy would slowly recover, found their hopes slipping away with the second wave. Many spoke of lingering fears and skepticism among foreign tourists about India's management of COVID, especially after the second wave, and anticipated that they would not return in a hurry even if international flights resumed. Addressing this, Akaash said, "they [tourists] fear coming to India and getting sick or stuck here and to avoid this, are choosing to not travel."

Once it became evident that the pandemic's impact on the tourism economy would extend beyond the lockdown, aid and assistance among mutuals also dried up. According to Amir Sahab, a local leader-cum-hotel owner, many civil society organizations, local leaders and politicians, as well as one's family, friends, and acquaintances, had extended help with food,

---

4   Beginning in July 2021, the weekend lockdown was lifted, and the Taj Mahal is now open on weekends.
5   Day long trips where tourists come in to the city in the morning and leave by evening.
6   A popular north India tourism circuit comprising Delhi, Agra, and Jaipur.

money, and daily care, during the initial national lockdown. However, after the second wave, and with widespread lingering economic insecurities, community aid also slowly came to halt as everyone began to worry about saving for themselves and budgeting for their own futures and potential emergencies.

In August 2021, business, according to Umar (shop owner) and Faisal (tour guide), continued to be slow–hardly any customers and most did not make purchases or hire tour guides like they used to earlier. Trying to keep up with changing clientele, others, like Akaash (tour operator), attempted to cater to Indian tourists but did not find that to be fruitful because, facing their own economic uncertainties, big hotels and travel agencies had also drastically dropped their prices and were currently at par with boutique enterprises, like Akaash's agency and Amir Sahab's hotel. Naturally, tourists preferred these options that would otherwise be out of their budget.

State In/actions

Aside from shifts in tourists and their consumer behaviors, entrepreneurs also pointed to certain state-led (in)actions that they saw as decidedly hindering an already-flailing tourism economy. Mostly, these restricted opportunities for economic participation among local, ambulant entrepreneurs, especially tour guides and photographers who worked from outside the gates.

For example, the ticketing windows outside the west and east entrance gates of the Taj Mahal were closed during the lockdown period, and the move to digital and online ticketing – a long sought-after ideal – was finally realized. The windows remain closed till date, despite many entrepreneurs saying that tourists too were inconvenienced and frustrated by this: the Internet near the monument is weak, many tourists don't have smart phones or are not well-versed with the booking process. A nascent economy had burgeoned around this shift, where tour guides and small shop-owners would book online tickets for tourists in exchange for a small processing fee. Unsurprisingly, the police present at the gates had also begun to demand their "cut" from entrepreneurs who offered these services.

Entrepreneurs and local leaders, like Amir Sahab, were vocal in their belief that "*sarkaar* – different state agencies involved in tourism" – had mobilized the pandemic to their advantage to push for regulations that restricted entrepreneurial practices that they–the administration–deemed unsavory. In this vein, the digital shift for ticketing and the closing of the window was seen as regulating and deterring *"lapka"*[7] work from the gates, severely curtailing the economic conduct and viability of self-employed and ambulant tour guides, photographers, and hawkers and vendors, who capitalized on tourists waiting to buy a ticket to solicit their goods and services. These actors were already perceived as aesthetically displeasing to the local administration and tourists, and were frequently characterized in the vernacular media as engaging in petty crimes and aggressive pursuits of tourists, that harmed Agra's reputation and tourism (Bhandari 2021).

The pandemic had also seemingly provided an opportunity to state agencies to push for or experiment with regulations that they had long sought but unable to realize due to collective action from entrepreneurs. In this vein, the Archeological Survey of India (ASI) – an autonomous agency under the federal government tasked with managing heritage monuments and their upkeep – had been pushing for a cap on the number of tourists permitted inside the Taj Mahal for several years.

---

[7] A derogatory term used commonly to refer to the activities of ambulant, self-employed tourism entrepreneurs, like tour guides and photographers, who work from prime market spots, like the ticketing window and solicit their services to tourists. The term "lapka" references their competitive work actions–to jump up with the intention of catching tourists by out-competing others. For a more detailed discussion, see my earlier paper, *Talking Crime and Aggression* (Bhandari 2021).

It was briefly able to realize this when the Taj Mahal opened after the first lockdown, on September 21, 2020, with a limit of 5,000 visitors per day, in keeping with physical distancing norms (Divya, 2020). Although this cap has now been lifted,[8] an ASI official I spoke with mentioned that once tourists were back in full strength, the ASI would try once again, to reinstate a cap. Entrepreneurs too were worried that a precedent had been set that ASI would try to reinforce in the future.

The ASI had also, successfully and sans a paper-trail, regulated the entry of tour guides inside the monument; state-registered tour guides were the biggest losers. In Agra, there has been a long-standing conflict between federally registered and state registered tour guides over territorial control. The federal guides had petitioned in court that only they should be permitted to work in federally protected monuments, like the Taj Mahal, a litigation they had subsequently lost. As a federal body, ASI was widely perceived to lend its support to the case of the federal guides, and post-lockdown, many tour guides reported that the ASI gate attendants would target state registered tour guides and deny them entry, citing physical distancing norms. These measures either directly hindered some economic actors and their activities or at the very least, created an environment of uncertainty vis-à-vis regulations that could severely curb small-scale entrepreneurs' economic participation.

Pandemic Continuities–Lingering Uncertainties

Entrepreneurs also evoked the register of continuity when speaking of the pandemic's impact on their economic lives as a gradual move from uncertainty to precarity. State disregard towards tourism and its entrepreneurs was perceived to be a critical factor that engendered long-term uncertainty that had, during the pandemic, tipped entrepreneurs towards precarity. This state (in)action was characterized as typical, arising out of longstanding politics, implementation issues, and formulation of policies that didn't take into consideration views from the ground and were generally unsympathetic towards those affected.

"Sarkaar ne toh tourism ki taraf kabhi dhyaan hi nahin diya – the state never paid attention to nurture tourism" was a common refrain among entrepreneurs although they offered a variety of reasons for this. According to Akaash, the government benefited much more when big foreign or national companies set up businesses in Agra and therefore, had never really encouraged or supported local community–centered entrepreneurship: "the expectation was that we [local residents] would find work in tourism as employees–salesman, tour guide, hospitality workers; no one really saw us as business owners," he concluded. Another prominent tourism entrepreneur-cum-local leader surmised that the government had always treated tourism as a "cash cow" – an opinion he had articulated many years ago as well – and was happy to benefit from it but never really saw it fit to invest time or money into it.[9]

To relieve entrepreneurs' precarity during the pandemic, the federal government launched two loans schemes, specifically for tourism entrepreneurs. The Emergency Credit Line Guarantee Scheme (ECLGS) 3.0 was announced in March 2021 to "support eligible Micro, Small and Medium Enterprises (MSMEs) and business enterprises in meeting their operational

---

8   During the second wave, the monument was again closed to tourists between April-June 2021, and subsequently reopened with another cap–of 650 tourists inside the monument at any given time–although how this is managed and enforced is not clear (Al Jazeera 2021).

9   A few entrepreneurs believed that the pandemic had come at a time when the state and federal governments were already trying to de-legitimize Mughal and Muslim heritage as well as entrepreneurs; tourism entrepreneurship around the Taj Mahal entailed both these aspects, and therefore, the state was seen as not making any efforts to allay economic disruptions.

liabilities and restarting their business." By June 2021, a similar loans scheme—Loan Guarantee Scheme for Covid Affected Tourism Service Sector (LGSCATSS)–was launched to provide loans "...upto INR 1.00 lakh [each] to...Regional Tourist Guide/ Incredible India Tourist Guide approved/recognized by the Ministry of Tourism and Tourist Guides approved/ recognized by the State Govt./ UT Administration", to enable tour guides, "...to discharge their liabilities and restart their business affected due to Covid-19 pandemic."[10] However, entrepreneurs pointed out that in actual practice, banks were wary of giving loans, especially to tourism entrepreneurs, because there was no certainty of when their businesses would resume. Akaash also noted that many entrepreneurs were themselves wary of availing these loans because they did not know how long tourism would take to get back on its feet and didn't want to accumulate interest that they would have to pay out of their savings. These schemes also equated enterprise with those having a physical set-up, like small production units, shops, gyms and beauty parlors, and ambulant tourism entrepreneurs who provided services through guide work or photography, were not sure if they even qualified for these loans.

Entrepreneurs also bemoaned the fact that they did not get any tax waiver during the pandemic; this added to their expenditure despite a prolonged period of uncertain earnings, and pushed many towards non-compliance, leaving them vulnerable to future punitive actions by tax agencies. There was also no relief from everyday expenditure on utilities and rent, and at least three entrepreneurs–two shop owners and one tour operator–spoke of spending more money to keep their businesses afloat than they were earning. Amir Sahab blamed this on earlier state action of privatization of key services, like electricity. According to him, during the lockdown, the private electricity company kept sending bills and did not disconnect services for non-payment, as is the norm. These payments were now being enforced as entrepreneurs ostensibly returned to work, even as earnings remained highly irregular and restricted.

The failure of these state actions to alleviate entrepreneurs' economic precarity was attributed primarily to the fact that entrepreneurs – as intended beneficiaries – had not been part of the consultation process. When asked about the types of interventions entrepreneurs would have preferred, most overwhelmingly supported direct cash transfers, waiving off of utility bills, reduced rents, and healthcare insurance for COVID. Other indirect actions that could have a positive impact on work and earnings included weekend openings of the monument (in effect now from July 2021) and the reopening of the ticketing window (still not functional).

Entrepreneurial Anxieties and the Search for Alternatives

Addressing the looming economic uncertainty with no foreseeable end in sight, many entrepreneurs were looking for alternatives, but with varying measures of success. Many felt "trapped" and anxious and considered moving out of tourism but were unsure of what else to do. In Umar's words, "There is no guarantee that the new thing, whatever it is, will succeed. I would gladly love to move out of tourism but I don't have any options. *Na maintain kiya jata hai, na chhoda jata hai* – I cannot maintain it [tourism work] nor leave it. For now, I'm just sitting here, trying to minimize expenditure and praying for things to get better."

Akaash had shuttered his tour operator business "indefinitely" and moved back to run his family–owned shop at the west gate market, selling all and sundry tourism products and services such as, online ticket bookings to the Taj Mahal, guiding services, marble goods,

---

10 Government of India, Ministry of Tourism. Response in Lok Sabha to Unstarred Question No. 1158, Answered on 06.12.2021.

leather products, keychains, hats, and scarves. "I paid my employees half their salary for a full year, from March 2020 to March 2021, but when the second wave hit and it became evident that tourism wasn't going to resume any time soon in a profitable way, I had to let them go," he rued. Currently, they were a tour operator agency in name only: no employees, no office, and no clients. "I want to move out of tourism completely," he said, adding, "*Mann bhar gaya hai* – I have lost interest – I sell whatever will sell because I am looking to get out now. That is my only aim." Akaash planned to move to Malaysia and marry his girlfriend, and from there, reassess his work options. Amir Sahab too sold his share in the hotel to his partner, Raja, because he was not on board with the partner's push for renting hotel rooms on an hourly basis, worrying that these would foster the use of their hotel for sex and sex work. Not only would this arrangement damage his standing as a local leader but also entangle them in risky encounters with the police and local authorities. Amir Sahab mentioned his plans to become a full-time politician with a national-level political party that has a receding presence in the state, and hence, perhaps, easier to join. At the time of writing, he had been made the party's election committee chief for Agra city and was hopeful of getting a "ticket" to contest the upcoming state elections in 2022.

Looking Ahead

Envisioning their future, entrepreneurs were not particularly hopeful of a quick recovery for tourism but many felt stuck and did not know where to move without making a substantial and equally uncertain investment. Hence, many like Umar, stuck around, hoping for things to get better, and even others, like Akaash, who vehemently said that they wanted to move out of tourism, kept an eye on the condition and factors that could lead to tourism's recovery.

Among the (short-term) factors that could facilitate tourism's recovery, entrepreneurs keenly awaited the resumption of international flights and the steadying of domestic travel. The optimistic timeline was that if flights resumed by December 2021, tourism would subsequently pick up within 6-8 months; some were willing and able to wait out this period. Other measures included the opening of the Taj Mahal on weekends (this is in effect now) and the reopening of the ticketing window (that remains closed).

In addition, entrepreneurs also advocated for measures that either put money directly in their hands and in the hands of potential domestic tourists, or helped save entrepreneurs some money. In this vein, Amir Sahab argued for a version of universal income that would keep tourism entrepreneurs afloat. Universal income, he believed, would enable domestic tourists to resume travel that they were currently cutting back on because of their own economic uncertainty. All entrepreneurs near-unanimously suggested that payment of rent, utilities, and taxes ought to be reduced or completely waived off till the economy got back on its feet; Umar noted that landlords who would lose out on rental income could make up that money by way of universal income payouts. Akaash and Umar also suggested that complete health coverage for all during the pandemic would make a big difference—currently, entrepreneurs were seen as saving their last bits of money for any health emergency.

In addition to these short-term measures, entrepreneurs situated the pandemic's impact on their economic participation and earnings, on a continuum of years of state-led neglect. They were quick to note that long-term changes were needed, with requisite state support, to ensure not just tourism's recovery but the well-being of local tourism entrepreneurs, such as themselves, within it. In speaking of these measures, entrepreneurs envisioned their economic well-being beyond the pandemic-induced precarity to a sustainable mitigation of economic uncertainties that have been a part of their everyday economic participation since economic liberalization in India. From this perspective, the pandemic became an opportunity to reconstitute tourism in an inclusive manner.

Whistle stop trips and the fast exit of tourists from Agra, had always been a cause for concern for entrepreneurs, compounding their economic uncertainties and creating conditions for them to enter risk-laden and risk-reinforcing commission alliances (Bhandari 2017). Such mode of travel became even more dominant during the pandemic. To counter this, many opined that Agra ought to develop its own local tourism circuit, drawing in Mathura (a nearby town popular with Hindu pilgrims), Bharatpur bird sanctuary, and Fatehpur Sikri (another Mughal-era heritage town within 45 kms of Agra), as well as myriad local monuments in the city so that Agra's association with the Golden Triangle would not be a drain on the city's tourism economy. "Look at Rajasthan, they are selling sand," *Netaji*, a popular local leader noted, elaborating that the state was doing well because it promoted its state-centered and multipronged heritage–heritage, wildlife, arts and crafts–something that was currently lacking in Agra's tourism promotion and that needed to be developed.

Younger entrepreneurs reiterated an old proposition that the city's nightlife and cultural life be developed outside of its heritage. Making this argument, Akaash said, "currently, once the Taj closes at 7pm, there is nothing for tourists to do." He suggested the need for discotheques, bars and restaurants, and while older entrepreneurs have not been vocally in favor of this, many have begun to back the idea reluctantly as things that foreigners like to do. Umar also suggested the need to not just have monuments but also museums: "Agra has rich Hindu-Muslim heritage. This should be showcased in museums."

There was considerable support among entrepreneurs for cleaning up the Yamuna and developing boat tours of the Taj Mahal as well as a riverfront promenade that connected key tourism sites, like the Taj Mahal, Agra Fort, and Mehtab bagh. Prior to the pandemic, environmental degradation, most visible in Agra through worsening air quality in the winter and sustained year-long water pollution of the Yamuna River, was a major concern among entrepreneurs. They were cognizant of the steady erosion of Taj Mahal's foundation and the degradation its façade, and aware that foreign tourists were appalled and dissuaded by pollution, and that this had begun to negatively impact the city's tourism, that would threaten, in the long run, their very entrepreneurial existence (Datta 2018). Amir Sahab mentioned that he was pushing his political party to include pollution checks and the construction of the riverfront promenade in its election manifesto.

As entrepreneurs outlined these ways of developing Agra's tourism, they were quick to note that these plans must include and promote entrepreneurship among local communities and not just encourage big "outside" businesses to come in and take over. Some suggested ideas for this included having greater representation of local entrepreneurs in all tourism committees, and giving priority to community-owned businesses in any tourism development plans.

Concluding Thoughts

This paper offers some preliminary insights into how Agra's local, small-scale, and usually self-employed tourism entrepreneurs experienced the economic fallout of the pandemic. Already inhabiting an uncertain market and what they described as "risky business", most entrepreneurs felt a sharpening of their uncertainty and a rise in the risky-ness of their businesses. For many, like tour guides and photographers who worked from the gates, uncertainty transformed into economic precarity rather swiftly, forcing them back towards old strategies of economic diversification, that many had happily left behind or wished to leave behind. These diversification strategies signaled downward mobility and tourism entrepreneurs, ever cognizant of the promises of respect, free-will (*apni marzi se*), and creativity that tourism offered, found themselves back in jobs they disliked or had moved out of. Albeit those with savings continued to hold out and wait for tourism to recover, their anxieties were palpable as they slowly began to reckon with the possibility that the economy may take a longer time to recover than they could hold out for.

In what I can only describe as Agra's deeply encoded ethic of entrepreneurialism (shaped, in no small measure, around its tourism economy), many entrepreneurs were already on the move, working on their next venture. In this vein, Amir Sahab's move to politics must also be considered as a form of entrepreneurship – with a business he no longer wished to be associated with, he saw an opening to transform from a local leader to a local politician and was working on it as a career move. However, many, like Umar, also felt stuck: with tourism as the biggest employer in the city that had over time, decidedly negatively impacted other economic spheres (like the leather industry), many of Agra's residents did not know what else to do. And so, many continued to wait, stuck in a limbo where sales were few and far between and expenses ever accumulating. It is for this reason—the centrality of tourism to Agra's economy—that many entrepreneurs, despite genuine declarations of wanting an out, kept a side eye on the economy, looking for signs of life and revival.

However, what was of interest was that despite experiencing the disruptions of the pandemic as forms of economic rupture, entrepreneurs also underlined the continuity of their economic uncertainties.[11] They referenced state-led (in)actions and the lack of care towards engendering inclusive forms of community-centered entrepreneurship in Agra, and brought to the fore, the continuing, albeit reconfigured role of the state in the everyday practices of neoliberalism and economic liberalization (Gupta and Sivaramakrishnan 2011).

Over years of my research, local residents-cum-entrepreneurs have consistently complained that state agencies only envisioned them as workers and not entrepreneurs.[12] This sentiment was reiterated this time as well, and entrepreneurs spoke not just of general neglect and locally uninformed policies but of specific and targeted discriminatory actions, where the pandemic was mobilized to implement regulations that had previously been vehemently opposed by entrepreneurs. Most important among these were the digitalization of ticketing and the closure of the window that effectively killed a prime market spot for ambulant tour guides and photographers, and the practice of preventing state-registered tour guides from entering the Taj Mahal.

However, entrepreneurs also hoped that the pandemic could be a positive rupture where tourism and its entrepreneurial capacities itself could be reimagined in a sustainable and inclusive way. Inclusion of local communities, representation through stakeholders' committees, developing Agra's tourism in a holistic fashion to retain tourists for more than day-long visits, addressing environmental pollution, and designing waterway tours and tourism promenade with a clear allocation of shops and businesses to local and small-scale entrepreneurs, were

---

11 Cross (2010) makes similar observation in his work to characterize the experience of neoliberalism among shopfloor workers in southern India, as "unexceptional."

12 Ferguson and Gupta (2002) provide a theoretical framework to think of neoliberalism as a form of governmentality, while Galemba (2008) gives an account of how neoliberal economic formation characterize certain enterprises and entrepreneurs as illegal or illicit, that are then subject to governmental regulations and frequently, punitive action.

some measures that were mentioned.[13] As is evident, many of these were dependent on proactive and favorable state-led actions.

Zooming out from the specificities of Agra, I want to draw attention to the contradictions enfolded in small to medium forms of entrepreneurship in India. The ethic of entrepreneurialism is a familiar one in the country, articulated and commonly captured through the trope of *jugaad* or "making do," that is variously appreciated as an inherently Indian propensity for innovation and enterprise, derided for its short-cut approach and lack of rigor, or seen as exemplifying structural constraints to steadier forms of economic participation (See Jeffrey and Young 2014, Irani 2019, and Ghosh 2020). In the past decade, entrepreneurialism and jugaad have gained renewed valence, endorsed by the state and the political office-bearers as exemplifying self-reliance and success (Irani 2019). This discursive valorization has occurred in tandem with the slowing down of economic growth and job creation, processes that started before the pandemic and have been accelerated since. In this scenario, the endorsement of entrepreneurialism pins the responsibility on individuals to find suitable skill development and work opportunities for themselves by mobilizing their jugaad instincts, and enables the state to side-step its roles and responsibilities towards job creation, upskilling, and allaying economic uncertainty. However, my fieldwork among Agra's tourism entrepreneurs has consistently revealed that uncertainties and risks that beset their economic participation and inform their everyday economic conduct—from forging commission-based alliances to the adoption of aggressive persuasion tactics with tourists for shopping—are structural and often originate in the state apparatus, through policies, bureaucratic and administrative actions, and their everyday interactions with state agents, like the police. These in turn, reinforce a negative reputation for Agra as a tourist destination, and deepen the uncertainty and risky-ness of local tourism. Entrepreneurs have consistently outlined the need for state support to create structures where local enterprises are encouraged and included, and that Agra's tourism be given a direction in consultation with local communities and stakeholders.

This paper began with the intention to explore the possibilities of enterprise in the "new normal". However, conversations with entrepreneurs reiterate older and lingering concerns around Agra's tourism, primarily, the need for a state-supported environment where productive forms of entrepreneurship can foster. This preliminary research is an invitation to consider a more proactive role of the state in engendering entrepreneurship. In this respect, the pandemic and its ruptures do indeed provide an opportunity to move away from an individualized imagination of contemporary entrepreneurship that entails a constant, lonely hustle.

A Note on Methods and Data Collection: I had begun my dissertation research in Agra with tourism entrepreneurs in 2012 and continued to stay in touch with many of them through occasional phone calls to mark special occasions and festivities, and sometimes on a slow workday for one of us. More frequently, we stayed in touch via WhatsApp; I received many a "good morning" and other inspirational messages from a few entrepreneurs, we exchanged pleasantries and information about our lives. Once the pandemic began and India went into a national lockdown on March 22, 2020, my communication with Agra increased: we worried about health, complained about politics, shared statistics and stories on people affected

---

[13] For an account of successful community-participatory and state-led heritage tourism development, see Waters 2003.

with COVID, and slowly, we began to also talk about their work, concerns over the extending lockdown, and the fact that their earnings had come to a complete standstill. To a few entrepreneurs that I knew had limited resources and savings, I extended monetary assistance.

Over time, our communication altered in form: entrepreneurs, back in the market but without much work, began making group video calls on WhatsApp, that is, one entrepreneur would call, and I would see and speak to 4-5 of them who were sitting together. They always messaged before calling to ask if I was available. I reciprocated the same form. A few of them who wished to speak privately would make or request calls–phone audio, WhatsApp audio, WhatsApp video–usually on Fridays or Saturdays in the afternoon.

Once I began to consider doing this research, I reached out to different entrepreneurs, making individual video calls, seeking each one's participation and consent. Once agreed, data was collected mostly through individual video calls with 6 entrepreneurs, 2 local leaders, and one government official; among these, I spoke weekly with 4 entrepreneurs and 1 local leader. Group calls were only made if entrepreneurs initiated them. I sought permission to record, and some agreed on a few occasions. For the rest, I took shorthand fieldnotes that I later expanded into long fieldnotes. Formal fieldwork was begun in June 2021 and is ongoing.

CHAPTER 4

In Pursuit of Quality and Taste: Post-Industrial Entrepreneurs

ATAK AYAZ

Introduction

The question of where human beings began to cultivate grapes and drink wine is contested among archaeologists working on world wine heritage. Although newly discovered archeological sites have changed the final verdict on grape domestication, Anatolia is accepted as one of the birthplaces of *Vitis vinifera L* (Atalay and Hastorf 2006). In other words, grape cultivation and wine production have been an essential part of agricultural activities for the various civilizations established in Asia Minor and in the land that we call Turkey today (Corti 2017; Soileau 2017).

During the Ottoman Empire, the predecessor of the Republic of Turkey, there were various control mechanisms and legislations regarding the making and drinking of wine depending on the religious and ideological stance of the sultan in power. However, the literary and historical writings suggest that wine was consumed not only in the sultans' court but was also popular among soldiers and the peoples of the empire (Halenko 2017, Eldem 2017).

When we come to today's Turkey, wine has constituted a national(ist) project for the republic, especially during the early years after its establishment in 1923. In line with the state's secularist ideologies, grape cultivation and winemaking were heavily supported by the country's founders (Fatma and Suut 2000). As a republic founded on a statist economic model, production in various sectors was controlled and dominated by state-led investments. TEKEL (Turkey's state-monopoly) directed alcohol production with its large-scale facilities in multiple localities. As the result of a long research period run by (inter)national experts, the country was mapped based on soil (Biron 1948) and appropriate state investments made. Although the state-owned facilities constituted the biggest producer in Turkey, wine production was never totally monopolized. Starting in the republic's early days, wine was produced by state-owned facilities and private initiatives.[1]

Even though wine has been continuously produced in Anatolia and Thrace (the two regions that make up Turkey today) for centuries, the country is not accepted as a significant wine-producing location. Grape cultivation has always been an important economic and agricultural activity for Turkey, which is the fourth-largest grape-growing country globally. Nonetheless, the share of the cultivated grape in winemaking was as little as 3 percent in 2008; a significant quantity of grapes is used for the raisin industry, of which Turkey is among the top five exporting countries.

However, wine making in Turkey accelerated in the last decades. With the shift toward a neoliberal economy and TEKEL's privatization in 2004, investors and entrepreneurs have become more effective than ever in molding the wine-sphere, especially by producing quality-oriented bottles with a holistic approach embracing grape cultivation and winemaking. This new mode of production, which I call "post-industrial," only began in the late 1990s, blossoming subsequently in the first decade of the 2000s. In the last few decades, Turkey has been attempting to become a part of the wine world by following the quality-oriented model of production that started in European countries centuries ago, with U.S. wineries joining in the 1970s. As a result, data from the Turkish Statistical Institute reveal that the distribution of grapes has shown a significant change in recent years. As of 2017, 10 percent of the country's grapes have been used in winemaking; in 2020, it was 13 percent.[2]

To this end, the investment of elites are significant for comprehending the changing ecologies of production that have enabled the transition from industrial to post-industrial. While the former is based on volume, the latter primarily highlights the features of the final product. The change from industrial to post-industrial indicates a shift from quantity to quality; in other words, a quality turn is happening in Turkey's wineries. This does not mean that the wine previously produced in Turkey was of low quality. However, "quality" as an adjective was not a denominator for the production strategy.

To this end, this paper focuses on the ongoing changes in Turkey's wine sphere while providing a brief synopsis on grape cultivation and wine production in Anatolia. In recent years, many white-collar workers and economically advantaged people from Turkey's major cities are moving to the rural parts to establish their wineries. Scrutinizing the urbanites' motives for moving their capital to rural areas will help us conceptualize post-industrial entrepreneurialism and its features. Finally, I argue that closely looking at the new agrarian class active in setting the bar for quality of wine in Turkey is crucial for understanding how post-industrial production is spreading around the world and agrocapitalism is being reconstructed.

Post-Pastoral Sentiments

In her seminal book on artisanal cheese-making in the United States, Heather Paxson (2013) defines people who have left their jobs, apartments, and lifestyles in the city centers to produce artisanal cheese in small localities as "post-pastoral." Paxson's definition stems from the fact that these people do not see nature and culture in opposition to one another as in the classical

---

[1] Two of the leading wineries of Turkey were established in the early years of the republic—Doluca in 1926; Kavaklıdere in 1929.

[2] https://arastirma.tarimorman.gov.tr/tepge/Belgeler/PDF%20Tar%C4%B1m%20%C3%9Cr%C3%BCnleri%20 Piyasalar%C4%B1/2021-Ocak%20Tar%C4%B1m%20%C3%9Cr%C3%BCnleri%20 Raporu/%C3%9Cz%C3%BCm,%20Ocak-2021,%20Tar%C4%B1m%20%C3%9Cr%C3%BCnleri%20Piyasala%20 Raporu.pdf (Access Date: 01 February, 2022).

pastoral imaginary. Instead, they work in collaboration with organic agencies in a productive fashion: "Their ideological anchor is a revised pastoral that critiques industrial capitalism's wholesale exploitation of nature and culture yet retains, while modifying, an opposition between city and country—and it hopes to offer a better way forward" (Paxson 2013: 17). In other words, moving to rural areas for post-pastoral people does not only mean "escaping" from the bustle of urban life but also actively engaging with economic production in their new localities. This production differs from the classic capitalist mode, which mass produces identical products. Instead, post-pastoral producers (although they are still in the realm of capitalism) aim to produce locally in a sustainable and nature-friendly way that corresponds to artisanal production's ethical and cultural values.

Silvia Yanagisako argues that understanding capitalist selves, motives, and strategies that are shaped through peoples' (bourgeoisie or worker) everyday practices is significant for comprehending how capitalist societies function. In her ethnographic research on the silk industry of Como, Italy, she questions the "cultural sentiments, meanings, and subjectivities [that] motivate and shape entrepreneurial actions" (2002: xi), Yanagisako takes steps to recognize "how these individuals have arrived at the sentiments and desires that lead them to pursue the particular entrepreneurial projects that, in turn, have shaped both their families and the … industry" (2002: 4). However, instead of using "interest," which has been systematized and rationalized through numbers, Yanagisako provides her analysis through "sentiments," as a term "to bridge the dichotomy between emotion and thought" (2002: 10). These emotional orientations and embodied dispossessions that can create specific desires and social actions. It is such an approach that I practice in my research, which scrutinizes not only the economic actions that are made by people in the wine industry in Turkey but the economic and moral sentiments behind these decisions. By accepting taste and quality as driving sentiments, I explain how wine production in Turkey is being re-invented by post-industrial entrepreneurs.

In line with Paxson's conceptualization of the "post-pastoral," Turkey's post-industrial winery owners come from upper-middle classes and non-agricultural sectors. Whether or not they are initially from the small localities where they produce wine, almost all owners of post-industrial wineries in Turkey come from different occupations and only later become vignerons/winemakers or winery owners. After working in various professions, they decided to invest their savings in winemaking. Some of the owners have left their jobs (which are mostly in city centers and/or in international organizations) and have turned winemaking into their major source of income; for others, it has become a form of investment, an additional source of revenue alongside the profession they have been practicing for years.

Even though the industrial logic of economic productivity may not govern post-industrial entrepreneurship, the final products circulate as valued goods. In other words, whatever personal sentiments each post-industrial winery owner carries, their bottles still serve as commodities in the market. Thus, valuation and economic sentiments should be considered while conceptualizing the meanings of entrepreneurialism. To this end, by scrutinizing the economic values and personal sentiments that these people deploy, this chapter opens a space to understand the various driving forces and motivations behind the formation of post-industrial entrepreneurial selves.

Post-Industrial

It is quite common in the wine world scene to see people with substantial economic capital shift a part of their wealth to wineries and/or vineyards. Gerard Depardieu, George Lucas, and Iniesta are just a few celebrities who take part in wine production in various parts of the world.

However, the list is not limited to actors, movie directors, or football players. Businesspeople, doctors, lawyers, and those in other professions with substantial socio-economic capital develop an interest in grape cultivation and winemaking. Following this trend, Turkey's first small-scale and quality-oriented winery, *Gülor*, was established in 1998 by one of the wealthiest families in Turkey: the Sabancı family.

Gülor is one of the pioneer institutions that introduced the noble French vines to Turkey's wine industry. Along with Cabernet Sauvignon, Sauvignon Blanc, and Merlot, they began to cultivate Sangiovese and Montepulciano brought from Italy. As a mutual dream of Güler Sabancı—chairperson of the family-controlled Sabancı Holding, the second-largest industrial and financial conglomerate in Turkey—and her chemical engineer uncle Orhan Türker, the establishment of such a new business model ignited a fire in Turkey's wine industry. What Gülor introduced to Turkey's wine industry goes beyond bringing internationally recognized new grape varietals. They heralded the birth of a new mode of production in the country's wine industry: post-industrial.

As stated above, there has been wine production in Turkey since its establishment in 1923. However, unlike the quantity-oriented industrial wineries that agricultural families have run for generations, the post-industrial wineries like that of the Sabancı family have been established by urban people from the upper-middle classes and non-agricultural sectors such as textiles, banking, and technology.

"I always liked drinking wine"; "There was a winery near our home in California"; "I visited various wineries when I lived in France." These are just a few sentences that I heard from my Turkish interlocutors when I asked why they decided to produce wine. In addition to underscoring their interest in sipping fine wines, they explained how their transnational lives and connections influenced their decision to produce it. Above all, the most significant commonality among my interlocutors' narratives is setting quality as their production goal. They did not shift their capital to agriculture for the sake of producing just any wine; rather, they have formed their sentiments and motivations for wine production to make bottles that they would enjoy consuming themselves. Moreover, they wanted to make commensurable wine with their international equals. Thus, quality construction is crucial for understanding these post-industrial wineries' production philosophies and how they differ from their industrial counterparts.

The price of a bottle of wine, where it is produced, the quantity of production, the grape varieties used in winemaking, the origin of the grape, and the technical equipment used in wineries are some factors influencing how quality is defined. As a matter of fact, the term "quality" itself is not uniquely employed in the wine industry nor unique to food production. It is used widely in all kinds and modes of production. One can talk about the quality of plastic flowerpots produced in large factories and a dress sewn in a tailor shop. However, what differentiates these small-scale and quality-oriented wineries that I define as post-industrial is twofold.

Firstly, post-industrial wineries develop a holistic approach from the cultivation of the grapes to the bottling of the wine. Since high-quality ingredients (in the case of wine, grapes) are one of the first necessities for a satisfying result (Ulin 1996, Simpson 2011), especially when observing and controlling the whole process from vineyard to glass, wineries that accept post-industrialism as their mode of production begin their journeys by establishing their vineyards. Unlike most annual harvest crops such as barley, sunflowers, and wheat, reaching the first harvest requires some patience. It takes three to five years for a grapevine to develop its berries. Because turning raw land into a vineyard is a long process, most of my interlocutors started their journey by finding the appropriate soil for wine production. Thus, running soil and climate analyses was crucial for my interlocutors in their pre-production periods. By dissecting the features of the soil, they attempted to understand if the land was suitable for grape cultivation and to figure out the best grapes varietals for the given soil structure. For Meltem and her partner, who relocated to Turkey after selling a company they established in Silicon Valley, finding an area for their winery was a grueling process.

> We visited various towns/cities/areas of Turkey to find the best place for our winery. It was a process; we did not decide to buy this land [points at the vineyards through the window] overnight. As engineers, we used our knowledge to analyze. The statistics of the last twenty years from the meteorological office and the soil anaylsis reports from the general directorate of mineral research and exploration guided this process. Also, the soil characteristic of this area greatly resembles Bourdeaux: argillaceous and clayey. We knew that it would be a great place to make internationally commensurable wine.

After finding the field for the vineyards, evaluating microclimates, opting for the grape varietals, and orienting and spacing rows, the time for building a winery arrives. Following global trends, post-industrial wineries in Turkey are either found in the same yard as the vineyards—known as the French *chateau* production style—or in close vicinity. The physical closeness between vineyards and winery is crucial for processing grapes right after harvesting them. In doing this, they can keep the phenolic features of the grape that serve as the base for high-quality wine.

Apart from the holistic approach that starts with cultivating grapes, the second feature of the post-industrial mode is its scale orientation. The goal of post-industrial entrepreneurs is not to produce a great number of wine bottles. Instead, to be able to observe the development of taste and quality and to sustain the distinctive characteristics of their wines, they remain small- (to medium-) scale producers. Anthropologist Yuson Jung's research on the economic and cultural values in Bulgaria's wine industry reveals the significance of the scale and systems of value. During her fieldwork in Bulgarian wineries, Jung's interlocutor John, an American oak barrel manufacturer and bulk wine importer, explains the relationship between the scale and quality as such: "You can't produce both distinctive fine wine and good-quality wine (albeit indistinctive) under the same [large-scale] infrastructure. The orientations are just different: in terms of market, production technology, and even business philosophy!" (Jung 2016: 287). The production scale is essential for determining the economic, cultural, and ethical values that a winery can create. Given that the post-industrial mode of production positions itself as a manifest against the identical goods produced in big factories, scale of production, in and of itself important to consider.

"Boutique" as a term is overly used among Turkey's wine producers and consumers. In line with the French concept *"vigneron indépendants,"* a boutique winery refers to a production house that cultivates grapes in their estates and makes their own wine. Although it is primarily a scale-oriented term, it also carries quality perception in Turkey. As such, the new generation of wineries are mostly defined as boutique regardless of how and what they produce. However, there is no consensus as to what the term entails exactly; nobody clearly knows the scale limits of grape cultivation and wine production for a winery to be defined as boutique.

Thus, Turkey's wine industry hosts various examples when it comes to production scale. First, wineries that started their journey as industrial production houses. Although they produce millions of liters, with their various segments or different brand names, they aim to sustain the post-industrial mode through the quality and taste of their wines. A second example is the wineries that reached millions of liters only reecently. Although they started as small scale producers, with constant capacity increases over the years they reached the limits of producing millions of liters of wine per year. The third example, on the other hand, is those wineries that remain small-scale production facilities. They may have slightly increased their production capacity in the last years; however, they seek to not pass a certain threshold so as not to change their production philosophy. Even though they show different stance towards the production scale, the foremost commonality among them is not only producing wine but also cultivating grapes.

Wineries from these three categories explain their business maneuvers differently. For the first group, to produce high-quality wine, learning winemaking processes and developing the necessary infrastructure was the most essential. As Deniz, one of the biggest table wine producers in the northwestern Thracian region of Turkey explained, his new brand is ready for producing more high-end bottles: "There is time for everything. I have been making wine for more than ten years now. The infrastructure is ready. From now on, we will produce outstanding wines. There is no reason not to produce better quality wine. I have different vineyards; I work with wine masters; I have a sales team; the production facility is ready! So, why not?"

However, the line of reasoning used for production-scale is slightly different for the wineries that have massively expanded in the last years. Although they have started producing on a small scale, in order to fill the gap in the market for various segments they excessively increased their production capacity. During my repeat visits, I could converse with the oenologist at one of these wineries. Hasan, a Turkish oenologist who studied in Europe, claims that although they have increased their production capacity, they have maintained their post-industrial ethos. For example, he stated that they put grapes from different plots into different vats, to preserve "the essence of place/terroir" (Trubek 2008). In line with how they made wine in the first years of the winery, they still observe the development of their wine not only for the high-end but also for medium segments. He argues that regardless of the segment of their bottles, they do not produce identical bottles regardless of the harvest year—their bottles still carry a distinctive taste compared to industrial producers. When it was established, Hasan's winery produced only hundreds of thousands liters of wine. However, they make more than two million liters of wine now. As a result, they started to buy more grapes from other cultivators and increased the acreage of their estate vineyards to provide more grapes for the harvest period. Even so, to strengthen his claim that they still maintain the ethos of the post-industrial mode of production despite their increasing production capacity, Hasan underscores the significance of their estate vineyards:

> We should never decrease the percentile of grapes coming from our estate vineyards. If it happens, we will lose our control over production. Nevertheless, to keep a certain grape quality coming from other cultivators, we hired a new experienced agricultural engineer. By doing this, we know that there is no drastic quality difference between the grapes we cultivate and other vineyards' grapes. Recruiting a new person for this specific goal is also a part of the production chain.

The major commonality between the first sets of wineries is that the demand in the market has been determining their production strategies. However, contrary to wineries determining their capacity mainly through the wine market, there are some producers who prioritize their personal and cultural sentiments. Producers from this third group do not want to increase their capacity drastically. For example, one of my interviewees, Fatma, who has studied International

Relations and Diplomacy in France and completed a wine certificate program in the United States, has subtly criticized others producers who are not small-scale anymore and explicitly stated that her company is proud of sticking to its foundational rules. She said: "Our authorized production capacity is 160 thousand liters. However, we only produced 100-110 thousand liters in one year. We plan to increase slightly in the following years, but it will never exceed 200 thousand liters. If we went beyond this threshold, we would have to change our production methods." As a winery that produces wine only from grapes coming from their estate vineyards and pressing them just once to keep the utmost taste and quality, she is hesitant about the post-industrial qualities of the wineries that produce in massive numbers. She claims that it is not possible for wineries to follow the taste and quality development of grapes and wines, regardless of how many more people they recruit.

As a country attempting to re-invent its wine production in the nexus of quality, Turkey's wine producers interpret the role of scale differently. It is evident that the personal sentiments (such as locally producing and being just toward the natural world) and economic ones (the scale, sales, market formation, and economic values) are determinant in shaping the scale of wine production. Nonetheless, combining grape cultivation and winemaking, providing (at least a part of the) grapes from estate vineyards lies at the core of the post-industrial production.

Compared to what Yuson Jung experienced in Bulgaria, the producers in Turkey claim that they are more structured about their business models and different sets of values applied over the years. Yung's interlocutor, John, a seasoned entrepreneur with more than 20 years of experience in the wine trade, accepts wineries that want to protect both their quantity and quality at the same time as failed business models. He defines that as "overscaled and underthought" as they are neither creating economic value nor generating any of the cultural or ethical values often associated with artisanal production (Jung 2016: 287). However, Turkish wineries that fall into these three categories (initially big-scale producers, recent big-scale producers, always small-scale producers) claim that their business models have been shaped as result of considering various factors, such as the level of investment, what the market requires, and how they socially and politically imagine their production.

Investors or Entrepreneurs?

The arrival of March heralds the last days of winter pruning in vineyards. To prepare the plots for the upcoming harvest period, shoots are tied, planting is completed, and the soil is tilled and sometimes manured. Before spring fully arrives and the reawaking in the vineyards can be observed with the naked eye, vignerons prepare themselves for the end of the dormant season.

The transition from winter to spring marked a significant period for my field research, too. Besides working as a cellar worker in a winery in the northwest of Turkey, I visited other producers in the same region mostly during this period to see how they prepare themselves for the upcoming spring and subsequent harvest. Moreover, as the workload is less tiring than during harvest time, the beginning of spring was a significant period for me to conduct in-depth interviews with my interlocutors. Through my initial visits and continued communication with my interlocutors, I was hired to work in a post-industrial winery during my fieldwork. There, I had the chance to follow the whole production process from vineyard to glass. My invested labor and embodied fieldwork enabled me to observe the development of the quality-oriented wine industry in Turkey.

When I look over the narratives that I collected from the winery owners and winemakers, the winery in which I spent the substantial part of my fieldwork stands out as an odd element. Coming from a vigneron family background, being born and raised in the region, and having studied at a world-renown viniculture and viticulture program in the United States, the winemaker, Alpay, had an excellent command of the region's specificities and the principles of winemaking. Although he accumulated the necessary cultural capital to overcome the economic obstacles through his upbringing and educational background, he established his winery with the help of a number of investors.

Once or twice a year, Alpay gathers all the investors to present and explain how the winery functions, unless there is not an urgent agenda topic to discuss. Other than that, he is the decision-maker when it comes to the volume of production, type of wine (red, white, or rosé), or which grape varietals to process. These people, called "angel investors," collect their profit some years after the establisment of the winery.

However, this is not how most of the post-industrial wineries in Turkey are established. A majority of them have formed their production houses primarily through the (family) money they accumulated over the years. To learn how to make quality-oriented wine, they either complete certificate programs/degrees in different parts of the world and/or collaborate with (inter)national wine consultants. Although some of these winery owners take an active part in collecting and processing grapes and bottling wines, some are primarily responsible for promoting the bottles rather than being a part of the entire production process. Considering that the wine industry in Turkey hosts people with different economic power, wine knowledge, and winery owners who invest various levels of physical participation, I had difficulties categorizing my interlocutors throughout my fieldwork. Although my research began with probing why and how they shifted a part of their investments into winemaking, I was not unsure whether to describe them merely as investors.

To have a field-oriented categorization and be fair to my interlocutors' labor, I asked them how they categorize themselves—or whether they call themselves investors. During one of these conversations, while we were discussing how risky it can be to earn money from the soil, one of my interlocutors, Fatma—whose family accumulated its capital primarily through tourism—explained in a detailed fashion why they do not define themselves simply as investors.

Atak: In recent days, I have asked the same thing to many investors: Is it risky to earn money from the soil? How do you read this?

Fatma: It is risky. Very! However, we do not see ourselves as investors. If we were mere investors, we wouldn't do this job. This is not something that one could do with a mere investment mindset. The investment mind would say 'No, it doesn't make sense to put money into this, as the moment of breaking even happens twenty five years later. The first generation doesn't even see it. I don't think that it is perfectly fine to call [us] investors. Because it is not something you would start doing with that mindset. Nobody would.

Atak: Okay. Then, how do you call yourselves?

Fatma: We say we are grape cultivators, winemakers. We are not only producing wine and cultivating grapes here. We started this to build a future-oriented model. Yes, we are doing monoculture. Yes, we have big vineyards, but there are oak tree and lavender gardens among vineyards. We try to have sustainable production by having things that support each other. We accepted a production method that doesn't leave any trace in nature and on the product. These are not decisions that no "sane investors" would make. We made these decisions with different motives. The climate crisis is real; this is not climate change.

And we are a part of this crisis. Now we are at the beginning of it, not in the middle yet. Although we are at the beginning of the crisis, it still holds some serious indicators. When we started this business years ago, we first discussed how we'd like to leave traces in nature. This is quite different from an investor's point of view.

As if corroborating Paxson's classification of the post-pastoral, Fatma fiercely defended that her ideological anchor is a determinant in defining how she structured her business model. As someone cautious about the environmental and climatic crises we are experiencing, rather than accepting a ruthless form of capitalism that utterly commodifies nature, Fatma explains how her moral sentiments have been determinant in the mode of production in her family's winery. Her desire lies in producing in an environmentally friendly manner that requires a limited amount of production. Thus, her production philosophy contradicts with the main doctrines of classical capitalism. Yet she still acknowledges that what they have done is indeed investment, even though they do not run their business openly through a mindset of a capitalist investor:

> *Fatma:* Of course, we are investors. In the end, we engaged in an investment here. However, it was not done merely through the mind of an investor. Otherwise, doing this would make one a bad investor. It would be an oxymoron [she laughs]. Is this a wrong investment? Absolutely not! If you only look through moneymaking, you would love to return the money.

Such conversations with my interlocutors pushed me to conceptualize their choices more as entrepreneurship. Their entrepreneurial selves go beyond having a command over substantial economic and cultural power. Along with taking part in grape cultivation and wine bottling, these people are also in charge of selling and promoting their bottles. These entrepreneurs have not solely shifted their capital but they also altered their lifestyles. While investors may visit wineries periodically, control how operation goes, taste the wine produced in the facility, and provide some necessary suggestions, they chiefly continue with their old lives in city centers. These entrepreneurs in Turkey, on the other hand, establish a new life in the localities where they have shifted their capital. On top of controlling production from vineyard to glass, they feel the necessity to find a new formula for their lives. Some of them have moved to locations where they produce the wine; some of them keep their houses in city centers and frequently commute to their wineries. Thus, the lifestyle changes they go through makes me read my interlocutors as entrepreneurs rather than mere investors.

However, regardless of how I describe their initivates, these post-industrial agents are altering not only the mode of production but the pastoral landscape. While long-term residents of rural areas are abandoning agriculture as it becomes less and less economically viable, well-educated urbanites from the upper-middle classes and non-agricultural sectors appear as the central actors behind cultivation and production. Thus, closely looking at the trajectories of the actors behind the post-industrial bottles is essential for comprehending the ways in which these producers are in pursuit of taste and quality, and how the agrocapitalism is being reshaped.

Conclusion

Based on my ethnographic research, the interactions I had with customers, and the interviews I conducted with winery owners and winemakers in Turkey's northwest, I argue the following: Turkey's wine market is in a constant state of re-making due to the new post-industrial mode of production and changing regulations and legislation pertaining to alcohol production.[3] However, the principles of being post-industrial constantly alter, depending on producers' personal sentiments and the development of Turkey's wine market. Therefore, it is a challenging task to draw a line between who produces in a post-industrial fashion and who does not. The lifestyle changes that wine entrepreneurs dream about and go through is important to consider. On top of *what* they produce, the question of *how* they produce also determines their entrepreneurial selves.

Producing high-quality wine stands as a noble form of agriculture for many in Turkey. As one of my interlocutors who is an environmental economist and owns a winery stated, "Wine is a great medium for those willing to pose as western and aristocract. It gives you the specific subject that makes you distinct from others. I believe that most of the boutique producers gravitated into its power." In line with her sentences, what my interlocutors do goes beyond restructuring the agrocapitalism in the nexus of quality, but they also reconstitute their identities through various forms of capital (Bourdieu 1986). Thus, delving into personal sentiments along with economic ones stand very crucial to interpret the restructuring of the capitalist selves and the mode of production.

In dwelling on the changes in Turkish winery owners' professional lives and their motives for bringing their capital to rural areas, this paper inquiries into how small-scale, quality-oriented production has restructured entrepreneurialism and agrarian capitalism more broadly. By centrally situating the roles of urbanites in these new openings, I claim that in the coming decades the recalibration of agrarian capitalism will create a paradigm shift in social stratification and inequality, the question of the peasantry, and (internal) migration.

References Cited:

Biron, Marcel. 1948. *Avrupa* Üzüm *Cinslerinin Türkiye (Trakya) Iklimine Intibaklari Acclimatization of European Grape Varieties in Turkey (Thrace), 1937 - 1947*. Istanbul.

Bourdieu, Pierre. 1986. "The Forms of Capital." Essay. In *Handbook of Theory and Research for the Sociology of Education*, edited by John G. Richardson. New York: Greenwood Press.

Corti, Carlo. 2017. "Wine and Vineyards in the Hittite Kingdom : a Case Study of Northern Anatolia and the Southern Black Sea Coast." In *Of Vines and Wines: The Production and Consumption of Wine in Anatolian Civilizations through the Ages*, edited by Thys-Şenocak Lucienne. Leuven: Peeters.

Doğruel Fatma, and Doğruel A. Suut. 2000. *Osmanlı'dan Günümüze Tekel*. İstanbul: Türkiye Ekonomik ve Toplumsal Tarih Vakfı.

Eldem, Edhem. 2017. "A French View of the Ottoman-Turkish Wine Market, 1890-1925." Essay. In *Of Vines and Wines: The Production and Consumption of Wine in Anatolian Civilizations through the Ages*, edited by Thys-Şenocak Lucienne. Leuven: Peeters.

Halenko, Oleksandr. 2017. "Wine in the Public Discourse and Banqueting Practices of the Early Ottomans." Essay. In *Of Vines and Wines: The Production and Consumption of Wine in Anatolian Civilizations through the Ages*, edited by Thys-Şenocak Lucienne. Leuven: Peeters.

---

3   In order to keep the coherence of the text, I have not delved into the legislations pertaining to alcohol production and consumption in this chapter.

Jung, Yuson. 2016. "Re-Creating Economic and Cultural Values in Bulgaria's Wine Industry: From an Economy of Quantity to an Economy of Quality?" *Economic Anthropology* 3(2): 280–92. https://doi.org/10.1002/sea2.12057.

Paxson, Heather. 2013, *The Life of Cheese Crafting Food and Value in America*. Berkeley: University of California Press.

Simpson, James. 2011. *Creating Wine: The Emergence of a World Industry, 1840-1914*. Princeton, NJ: Princeton University Press.

Soileau, Mark. 2017. "A Vinicultural History of Tur 'Abdin'." Essay. In *Of Vines and Wines: The Production and Consumption of Wine in Anatolian Civilizations through the Ages*, edited by Thys-Şenocak Lucienne. Leuven: Peeters.

Trubek, Amy B. 2008. *The Taste of Place: A Cultural Journey into Terroir*. Berkeley, CA: University of California Press.

Ulin, Robert C. 1996. *Vintages and Traditions: An Ethnohistory of Southwest French Wine Cooperatives*. Washington, DC: Smithsonian Institution Press.

Yanagisako, Sylvia Junko. 2002. Essay. In *Producing Culture and Capital: Family Firms in Italy*, xi. Princeton: Princeton University Press.

CHAPTER 5

Pitching Hype: Storytelling and Entrepreneurship

ANGELA K. VANDENBROEK, Texas State University

Pitch

At a Stockholm-based entrepreneur meetup, two entrepreneurs stood on stage ready to pitch their startup to a panel of venture capital investors (VCs).[1] The man tapped the laptop on the podium to display their first slide—a large image of their logo. "Hello! I am Per and this is Jonna and this is our startup, Forests! We are on a mission to understand the world's forests and their inhabitants." Jonna, in contrast to Per's typical entrepreneurial energy, moved to the second slide and told a somber story about a forest-dwelling species endangered by climate change. Continuing the somber tone on the next slide, Per talked more specifically about the importance of the world's forests in combatting global climate change. Over the course of my year of anthropological fieldwork in Stockholm's startup ecosystem, I attended just under 200 public startup pitches. This one fell in the middle of that year, so from that experience, I expected their next slide to swing back to the ebullient tone of their introduction as they presented a "solution" to the "problem" they had just laid out—following the problem-solution narrative that dominates technology entrepreneurship and design (Pink et al. 2020; Morozov 2013). This was a common pitching tactic. Yet, on the fourth slide the endangered animal appeared again. In an exaggerated tone of exhaustion the event's host interrupted, "Oh, this guy again!" The entrepreneurs laughed nervously, skipped the remainder of the slide and returned to their scripted pitch. Their pitch was for a social logbook mobile app for birders, amateur naturalists, and other forest enthusiasts that crowdsourced data for climate research. Although, before they could get much further than this brief explanation the moderator interrupted again: "Let's pause there because I think we are about to get to the good stuff. But, that was a very lengthy Swedish introduction!"

---

[1] This story has been anonymized, including names and some details of the pitch.

Swedish entrepreneurs were frequently teased or ridiculed for their stereotypical inability or aversion to hyping like their American counterparts. Swedish and Scandinavian cultural concepts like *jantelagen* (the law of jante, social norm of humbleness and rejection of personal aggrandizement) or *lagom* (not too little, not too much) were used to explain the social norms of humbleness and care for community over individual achievement among Swedish entrepreneurs—qualities that were perceived as something that must be overcome to become successful entrepreneurs. The Forests pitch with its focus on impact, community, and care typified what was commonly critiqued as a "Swedish" pitch.

These public pitching events before panels of VCs at meetups, conferences, and competitions were touted as a way to showcase upcoming entrepreneurs who had been curated by event hosts and as a "peak behind the curtain" into the pitching process and the minds of investors. I attended these events with fellow audience members consisting of various ecosystem stakeholders, including aspiring entrepreneurs, established and serial entrepreneurs, other investors, entrepreneurial educators and mentors, employees from Sweden's many business-related agencies, among others. Through these events, we learned how to "properly" hype products, startups, and ideas. From public pitches to educational programming at universities, incubators, and accelerators to informal mentorship and casual advice, hyping is taught as a skill essential for entrepreneurial success.

However, hype was not a simple tool, beloved by entrepreneurs. Rather, it was a much maligned, often ignored, tactic for telling stories that enrolled allies in one's ambitions and projects—allies who could contribute financial or material resources; advice and guidance; expertise, time and energy; their networks and audiences; and so on. Hype was the connective tissue of entrepreneurial projects, holding people and materials together and propelling

A panel of venture capital investors at STHLM Tech Meetup, one of Stockholm's meetup events that features public pitching. (Image by Author)

them along common trajectories. Yet, the power and influence of hype storytelling was lost and obscured within discourses that perceived hype as a cynical form of aggrandizement that chafed against Swedish social norms. This allowed practices of hype to be diverted toward the needs, interests, and desires of a handful of actors within the community—most notably VC investors.

Hype Storytelling

SthlmTech, Stockholm's startup ecosystem, is saturated with hype. Sweden and Stockholm's public diplomacy organizations hype local innovativeness across history from Nobel's dynamite to the founding of Spotify. Evangelists, investors, and other ecosystem leaders spend large amounts of time promoting SthlmTech, its startups, and inventions—through the production of events, showcases, and media. These promotional efforts are not only meant to create general and political support for SthlmTech but also to drive people toward its innovation curriculum for generating the futures its leadership hope to bring about though it. Hype storytelling is a key feature of SthlmTech; yet, one largely unappreciated.

> I'm upset that the media, sometimes in Sweden, will hype up anyone. They hype up someone who just started—before they have made something. It is not the right thing. You cannot celebrate before you achieve something. You have to earn it a bit. I get pissed off when I think about it. I know a lot of people who are suffering to do something that will really make a difference in the world. That is what entrepreneurship is all about. That is why real founders exist. Not because they want to be cool or known.

As evangelist and entrepreneur, Maral Kalajian[2] expressed in this interview with me, hype was not something that was appreciated by the people I talked to in SthlmTech. The primary reason was because most associated it with the practices of so-called wantrepreneurs—that is a mythical type of American-style entrepreneur who was known for seeking a glamorous "entrepreneurial" lifestyle that included a lot of press coverage and morally, ethically, or socially poor ideas for startups—if they had an idea yet at all. Adil, a Palestinian-Swede and founder of an education-tech startup, told me that he "suffered" for his startup. As far as I know Maral and Adil did not know each other. However, I am confident that Adil would have easily fit Maral's understanding of what a "real entrepreneur" is. He worked long hours, was passionate about his work, was inspired by his personal struggles within education, and developed a service that aims to do social good. He was not likely to be found seeking out the spotlight unless it furthered his startup's cause. And, he too had a distaste for hype.

> Being a rockstar in the 80s, it was cool as a motherfucker. And that's being an entrepreneur today, right? It is so hyped up, so cool, so this, so that. I hate it. It's going to fuck up a lot of things for a lot of people. People think its cool, but... I guess the only message I want to get out, the only thing people need to know about taking on this role as a founder or co-founder is that it takes work. [...] You need to have a disgusting work ethic. You have to burn and have a passion for what it is you do. [...] Just work. That's my only thing I want to emphasize to all the bullshitters out there.

---

2 At the request of Maral, I am using her real name. Adil is a pseudonym, at his request.

This wantrepreneur phenomenon was generally attributed to changes in the media coverage of entrepreneurship in Stockholm and globally. Entrepreneurs went from being seen as barely employed wishful thinkers who sometimes achieved some level of success in business prior to the 2000s to potential "rockstars" after—with fan bases who read their books, attended their talks, dreamed of working for them, emulated them, or mourned them when they passed—like Steve Jobs, Mark Zuckerberg, Elon Musk, and Jeff Bezos—or, closer to SthlmTech, Daniel Ek (founder of Spotify) and Niklas Adalberth and Sebastian Siemiatkowski (cofounders of Klarna). Even new entrepreneurs with small, emerging startups could be rockstars if the right person spoke publicly about their potential. Most entrepreneurs and investors, however, disliked this rockstar status—even while using it for their own benefit—and foresaw a coming reckoning for the bubble created by the hype of rockstar entrepreneurs and by hyping entrepreneurship as the business of rockstardom.

Hype has a "tendency toward excess" that casts it as "a perjorative, a cacophony from which most people want to distance themselves" (Powers 2011, 217). During my fieldwork, discussions about hype were often bogged down by conceptions of hype as cynical, false, or deceptive speech or rhetoric. These discussions were focused on the quality of hype speech— its allure and honesty or lack thereof—in specific instances—as in "That pitch was just so over the top!"—or as a genre of speech—as in "Hype is such a distraction from real entrepreneurship." I describe these conversations as being bogged down because they elicited intense emotional responses from the people I talked to making it difficult to discuss hype beyond these particular, ubiquitous critiques.

Another feature of these conversations was a suspicion about my motives as a scholar. The people I spoke to were aware of the scholarly critiques of technology and startup hype as techno-utopian (Segal 1985; Hand and Sandywell 2002; Turner 2010; Poggiali 2016) or as techno-solutionism (Morozov 2013; Tiso 2013; Maturo 2014; Easterbrook 2014)—particularly as these critiques have become pervasive in popular media and blogs and were discussed in terms of Gartner's "trough of disillusionment" (Fenn and Raskino 2008) on popular technologies like AI and cryptocurrency. This suspicion was clearly manifested when, after asking an entrepreneur, Harry, if he would be willing to sit down for an interview, he said, "You won't catch me up. I'm not one of those people who buy into all this hype. So, I'm a bad person to interview." He became a semi-frequent conversation partner at events and on walks to the T-bana (Stockholm's subway system) after them. He even attended a workshop I hosted. He never did sit for an interview, however, as I was never able to convince him that my research was not seeking to call out "those kinds of entrepreneurs" for their naivety, neoliberal sentiments, or attraction to spectacle—I suspect that I also did not convince him that this isn't what I should have been doing.

After some time in the field, the swift and decisive ways that hype was dismissed as a topic to reflect on appeared to me glaringly incongruous with the pervasiveness and intensity of hype's presence across SthlmTech. If hype is devalued by the people of SthlmTech, then—I felt compelled to ask—why does it permeate so much of their everyday practice? To answer this question, it becomes important to understand that hype is not simply a cynical form of aggrandizement but also, as Kaushik Sunder Rajan found among biotechnology companies in Silicon Valley, hype is a promissory discourse in a speculative marketplace that calls "the future to account for the present" (Rajan 2006, 116). Setting aside the cynical perspective on hype, he argues that hype is a credible, fabricated truth that entrepreneurs and investors work toward rather than a fabricated lie that is meant to defraud and deceive. In this way, hype becomes a way for imagining the future and working to enact that future. The exaggerated tones and

A panel at FemTech listening to a pitch at another of Stockholm's meetup events that features public pitching. (Image by Author)

claims of hype are, then, tools for enrolling allies and securing investments (Brown 2003, 6). From this perspective, hype and expectations are performative measures for enacting an imagined future rather than a description or prediction of it (van Lente 2012). Thus, the measure of hype is not about "truth or falsity; rather it is about credibility and incredibility" (Rajan 2006, 114)—that is, one need not believe that the claims of hype will definitely come to fruition, only that it credibly could happen. Thus, hype is a powerful tool for enrolling allies in one's projects and ambitions for the way that it generates exciting, actionable knowledge—that is then tied to a prescribed and accessible practice for action.

Counter-Pitch

At the end of the pitch, the entrepreneurs lavished over their team's (and not their own) achievements and then displayed a QR code and short URL for the audience to download the app. At least half of the 200 or so attendees lifted their phones to capture it. Although they were mostly entrepreneurs and other entrepreneurial stakeholders, they were also predominantly Swedes—people from a country that has been repeatedly ranked as the most sustainable country in the European Union and the world, who have the legal right to wander in Sweden's forests (*allemansrätten*), and who repeatedly told me *"Det finns inget dåligt väder, bara dåliga kläder"* (There is no bad weather, only bad clothes) when I protested about winter's cold or summer's endless sun. For this audience, Forests's hype story was well matched to their interests and concerns.

The moderator asked the panel of Swedish venture capital investors, "What is going through your mind now? I would guess: How do they make money?" The first investor said, "I still, I just, I don't know *what* they do." The second, with a bit less incredulity added, "I guess I don't know what exactly they are collecting, what they are collecting it for, or how they will make money from collecting it." After a brief pause, the first investor said, "Ok, so this is like social media for hikers. I like that. It seems like a nice app. And, I guess you would be collecting a unique data set that no one else has. And, that gets me excited because as soon as you have unique data you can always use it for something. But then, I guess this is where I struggle. I don't get why this data is important. I get that this data is important for conservation which I think is great. But, how do you go from having that data to having an impact *and* making money from it."

Forests' cofounders had hyped their app well to the audience. In addition to the many who downloaded the app from their seats, the idea and its presumed necessity in regards to climate change were a popular discussion at the after-event mixer. Yet, the investor panel was unsatisfied. One of the VCs on stage, sensing the unease generated by a failed public pitch, said,

> This has potential, especially the social layer, that could be your unfair advantage over competition and copycats. But, you've told me a nice story about conservation today. And, that is not what I as an investor need to hear, even if I agree with you. What I need to hear is the core of your business; the conservation is a nice side effect that you can mention on the side. But, I need to hear about the core of your business.

The moderator, attempting to clarify for the entrepreneurs, explained,

> What's happening here is that you want to create this business because of conservation—and kudos to you for doing that and I hope more startups do things like this where they try to solve real fucking problems. Seriously, climate change is a huge fucking problem and we need people to do this. You can see that this is really driving them. But, that takes away from the potential of being a good business pitch. An investor has to know how they are going to get their money back. Those things can go together, but you have to understand your motivations are different.

"Look," the moderator said while turning around in his chair to face the entrepreneurs, "this is what you should say. I've built a great app that people love to use. It's a digital record book for hikers, birders, whatever, it has social stuff, gamification, it's addicting, people want to pay to use it. How do I know? Because we already have ten thousand users. And, hey, we can also use the data from it to save the planet by giving it to scientists." One of the investors pointed at the moderator and shouted, "Yes! I would give you money for that."

The hyped story of an app that could gather an unprecedented volume of urgent data to fight climate change was being evaluated by who the hype story is capable of enrolling as allies—that is people with a sense of climate change's urgency and whose priority and responsibility is to address that urgency—not venture capitalists. VC investors have a fiduciary and professional responsibility to grow their fund through investments that will scale their valuations exponentially over the term of investment. Even VCs who care deeply about climate change have little to offer as an ally on that matter alone. Rather, what VC allies can offer is expertise, resources, networks, and funds that support a company's *growth*.

Venture Capital

Venture capital is a form of capital invested in high-risk ventures. Venture capitalists, then, are the general partners and employees of a venture fund's management company. Venture capital is structured around a fund, a management company, limited partners, general partners, and their portfolio of startups. The fund is a pool of capital usually created by institutional investors, such as pension funds, insurance companies, or endowments; it can also include individual investors. This fund is structured as a limited partnership with the limited partners providing the fund and the general partners taking responsibility for the management company. The management company oversees the investment decisions and work to ensure that investments make returns, as they carry a fiduciary duty to their limited partners.

VC firms and the professionals that work within them invest in risky, but potentially high yield, ventures such as startup companies. This investment is usually an equity investment where the VC purchases common or preferred stock in the company, usually with liquidation rights to ensure a higher priority payout if the company fails. The fund makes money, then, when the company makes an exit either through an initial public offering (IPO) on the stock exchange, an acquisition by another company, or if the shares are purchased by another party, such as the founders or a new investor. However, the high rate of failure among startups means that a large portion of these investments (between 70-75 percent according to the VCs I spoke to) will never exit. This means that the fund is largely grown by a fraction of investments that have a "hockey stick" shaped growth pattern and are able to exit between $100 million and $2 billion, thus making the large failure rate viable in the long term.

Nearly all of the VCs that I spoke to referred me directly to or quoted without citation Steve Blank, a veteran serial entrepreneur from Silicon Valley and a prolific author and educator on innovation and entrepreneurship, for their go-to definition of a VC-friendly startup. Blank defined six types of startups, only one of which he identified as the kind of startup that works best with venture capital: the scalable startup (Blank 2013). The scalable startup accord-

A panel of investors at Stockholm Entrepreneurs, another of Stockholm's meetup events that features public pitching. (Image by Author)

ing to Blank is a "temporary organization in search of a scalable, repeatable, profitable business model" (Blank and Dorf 2012, 12). Or, in the words of one VC interlocutor, "Venture capital works best with small startups that look in the mirror and see the billion-dollar unicorns they will be in ten years—even if that is laughable. We don't play well with little shops that look in the mirror and are happy with their current reflection."

Unlike publicly traded companies, privately held startup companies have no external economic valuation measure and many lack revenue. Startups acquire valuations only when specific transactions occur, such as new investments. As privately held companies, they do not have the same obligations for reporting that publicly held companies have, making these valuations hidden from public view and determined by a small number of private individuals who make these decisions on a largely subjective basis (Miloud, Aspelund, and Cabrol 2012; Röhm et al. 2018; Köhn 2018). Bloomberg reporters Sarah Frier and Eric Newcomer (2015), based on interviews with VCs, described these valuations as "made-up" and dependent on investors "FOMO" (fear of missing out). This has made venture capital particularly dependent on VC-friendly hype storytelling for investment strategy and grooming entrepreneurs to tell these stories to them via participating in public pitching events, advice whitepapers and blogs, personal mentorship, interviews with journalists and other such venues.

Diversifing Hype Stories

Hype, I was told by entrepreneurs, was something that "had to be done" to achieve one's goals and get the necessary funds to continue. The term was used almost exclusively to describe the kind of storytelling that was valued by venture capital investors (e.g,. promotion of specific technologies, growth potentials, and potentials of achieving the coveted unicorn status) and typified by stereotypes of American, Silicon Valley entrepreneurs. It was almost never used to describe the storytelling valued by entrepreneurs as part of expressing their missions, goals, and solutions. Both of these, however, I argue are hype storytelling. The difference lies in how and who the stories attract and inspire.

With claims of "addicting" technology, large paying user bases, and "social stuff," the host's counter hype story had all the hallmarks of successful VC-friendly hype. Here, the moderator taught the entrepreneurs on stage and those in the audience how to construct a hype story that met the expectations of the VCs by foregrounding their values and needs and thus was capable of enrolling them as allies in the startup. Yet, problematically, because the entrepreneurs perceived this new story as hype and the former as a mission, vision, or goal, the nuance of how hype is used to enroll different allies is lost. Instead, the entrepreneurs, through these events, are taught that to be successful and valued within the entrepreneurial community, the VC-friendly hype story was the correct, best, and (to a certain extent) the only way to tell hype stories about their startup. Perhaps more problematically, I found that other types of investors (such as public organization fund managers, grant reviewers, private monetary award judges, and so on) had also adopted VC-friendly hype stories—their tropes, affinities, and rhetoric—as part of their assessment for investment. "I really like to attend the pitching events," a judge for a yearly award that provided seed funding for promising start-ups working in areas of social or ecological justice told me, "It's where I learn what's important and hot." I asked her if she was worried that this meant that her decisions were being unduly swayed by the logics and values of venture capitalists, which were not necessarily aligned with her organization's aims. She replied, "I don't think so. They are just our investment experts and so we listen to their advice."

Hype storytelling permeates entrepreneurial spaces, from startup mission statements and investor pitches to marketing campaigns and excited conversations over coffee. Unfortunately, the foregrounding of VC-friendly hype stories in entrepreneurial education—particularly at highly popular public pitching events—has erased other forms of hype storytelling from discourse on what hype is and what it is for. By generating and promoting this "correct" form of hype, the power of hype stories to enroll diverse allies is shrunk to the power to enroll specific allies, namely venture capitalists and others who share their values and needs. Meanwhile, potential allies who could provide alternative financial, material, or political support—that better align with the entrepreneurs' goals or could reduce reliance on less aligned allies—are often alienated by the rhetoric within VC-friendly hype stories or ignore opportunities that do not align with VC after also internalizing their hype education. This leads me to ask, in these spaces of entrepreneurship—where so much of our public and private resources, attention, and hopes are being diverted—how might space be created for alternative narratives (and education) that imagines hype as a tool for imagining credible futures with diverse allies aligned among common interests and goals? How might public pitching events for grant administrators or expert consultants generate different understandings about who startups could seek out as partners, advisors, consultants, or community allies? Lastly, how might this broader imagination of hype refigure the imaginations and assumptions of what startups are for, how they should operate, and what their priorities ought to be?

CHAPTER 6

Growth Hacking: On the Social Dimensions of High-Leverage Growth in Venture Capitalism

JAMIE WONG, Massachusetts Institute of Technology

The Art of Growth in a Gyroscopic Economy

In recent decades, the advent of the "startup" as a corporate form and cultural model has mythologized narratives of exponential growth. Startup founders, whose visionary leadership turns teams of a few loyal acolytes into companies valued in the billions in just a few short years, have become global celebrities and culture heroes. As advocates rally around imperatives of "disruption" and "innovation" and laud the technological conveniences and solutions that tech companies provide, critics have started interrogating the business models that allow them to grow with such speed. In particular, recent research has scrutinized how new logics of data accumulation influence the behavior of businesses and governments. As Sadowski writes, "Like finance, data is now governed as an engine of growth" (Sadowski 2019: 5). In current understandings of the political economy of big tech, data now features as a major source of value extraction (e.g., Zuboff 2019; Fourcade and Healy 2017), credited for having fueled the dramatic ascent of companies like Facebook, Google, Tencent, and Baidu.

Undoubtedly, data-driven digital technologies have allowed many of these businesses to enjoy lower marginal cost, faster business iteration, quicker expansion, and more diverse modes of monetization. However, I argue that explaining growth by technology alone may obscure important underlying social processes necessary for these businesses to capitalize on these technologies in the first place. Drawing on three years of fieldwork among Chinese startup entrepreneurs and the venture capitalists (VCs) who invest in their fledgling companies, I suggest that more attention should be paid to the socioeconomic reorientation toward what some among these actors refer to as "growth hacking."

There are myriad instructional books on growth hacking for business operations and marketing, but across different sub-domains, one core ingredient remains constant: "high leverage" (Fong and Riddersen 2017). "Leveraging" involves taking on risk and ceding control in order to do business with resources that one does not own for the sake of speed and flexibility. Traditionally, it often meant borrowing from the bank for one's business. Yet, VC promotes even more leveraging by allowing early-stage businesses that are often beyond banks' "risk appetites" to approach them for funds, not to be returned with interest later, but in exchange for shares in the company.

Arguably, the VC model's core "innovation" is for everyone involved from top to bottom to gain more leverage, in all different domains, to "grow" a business in the fastest way conceivable. Startups seek leverage, not only from VC funding, but also by outsourcing operations like computer programming, design, and manufacturing to jumpstart businesses at a speed they wouldn't be able to otherwise. As startup companies raise money from VCs, VCs court their own investors who provide the capital for further rounds of funds for the VC firms for whom they work. These investors include wealthy individuals, pension funds, university endowments, and the very corporate giants that startups are meant to "disrupt" through business or technological "innovation." Those who provide leverage expect a high reward for the risks they take (Nicholas 2019). This drives the entire system as a "gyroscope-like" economy that "cannot balance unless spun fast" (Xiang 2020). By requiring startups who take investment funds from VCs to chase "growth" at a pace that is not self-sustaining, the model makes them dependent on raising round upon round of investors' funds, without which they would perish.

To disentangle the social processes of growth hacking from the affordance of digital technologies for businesses (Sadowski 2019; West 2019), I analyze an ethnographic example from my fieldwork with a hardware startup. I argue that the accelerated growth of companies in recent decades that reach millions or even billions in valuation within a few short years is not solely a consequence of the advancements and mass adoption of data technologies, but requires coordinated social labor and temporal tactics. Through a comparison with trade practices among the Dobu, I demonstrate that growth hacking is not a novel social practice. However, its broad, coordinated adoption among startup entrepreneurs represents a significant new development in global capitalism, and necessitates novel interactional, organizational, and institutional frameworks that call for anthropological scrutiny.

Although it is impossible to explain the meteoric growth of startup companies without reference to technology, attributing too much explanatory power to technology alone risks contributing to teleological narratives of business evolution. In what follows, in the interest of illustration and the anonymity of my interlocutors, I create composite characters and companies drawing on my fieldwork in Shenzhen. This episode speaks to global trends as the model and logics of VC continue to spread into new economic and societal domains. However, it also reveals the kinds of locally specific entailments of domesticating the operations of the VC model, which, in the Chinese case, necessitate deep familiarity with what is locally understood to be guanxi (关系) practices, or "the art of social relationships" (Yang 1994). Guanxi, which directly translates to "relations," often refers to the ritualistic and performative maintenance of reciprocal relations that are integral to being a member of society (Yang 1994; Yan 1996; Kipnis 1997). By focusing on the social nature of the specific "techniques of time" (Bear 2016) in the Chinese startup sector, my analysis reveals guanxi practices for what they have always been – social means of seeking leverage – that participants in the VC model weave together with other high-leverage financial and technological practices to enact "growth hacking" as a cultural ideal.

Craft and Craftiness: Hacking for Leverage

Junyi did not set out to become an entrepreneur. It all started when he was working on a robotics project for class while in college in the United States, and one of his classmates and best friends applied for a school-wide startup competition on behalf of the group. Having glimpsed the world of VC through these programs, and spurred on by the promise of growing exciting businesses out of the robots they made, Junyi and his classmate began making robot prototypes to pitch to investors who could fund their business.

Over the course of a summer break while back home in China, Junyi finally caught the attention of one VC firm. It was one of the first crop of VC funds in China, established and managed by U.S. firms. Though an offer of investment was good news, Junyi still had some residual anxiety. Since President Trump's inauguration, U.S.–China relations had soured. Given this, Junyi did not know if it was advisable to take money from an American investor. What if his company, along with his U.S. investors, were boycotted as tensions continued to escalate? That would spell the end of a nascent business like his. As he conducted further research into this prospective investor, he found that they collaborated with various regional governments in China, including the one in his hometown. Local governments' willingness to work with these investors was a signal of trust and confidence from Chinese officialdom. Though not completely assured, Junyi thought that was sufficient indication that the VC firm was politically sanctioned to work with and decided to take a chance with them.

After taking the VC firm's investment, Junyi realized that these signals of "reliability" (靠谱) were not incidental. Many of the personnel at the VC firm laboriously cultivated these relations; for some staff, it was their entire job description. He was not the only one who was surprised. As some of his friends joined VC firms after graduation, they remarked that their work seemed to mostly consist of holding public events and building relations (打关系). One joked that they felt as though they had accidentally joined a PR firm. While all businesses engage in some form of public relations, what surprised these initiates to the Chinese VC community was the sheer amount of resources and labor poured into public facing events and public ties. Even when maintaining them was costly, precarious ties had to be painstakingly maintained. Its advantages, however, eventually became clear to Junyi as he benefited from his VC investors' efforts to maintain and grow their reputation and credibility as an asset (Helm, Liehr-Gobbers, and Storck 2011).

Junyi and his cofounder received what they felt to be a significant amount of money for a small stake in a startup company which did not yet have a saleable product. They soon became alarmed at the realization that they could only last for a few more months at their current "burn rate": the speed at which they were using up their liquidity as they hired new employees and prototyped iteration after iteration of their product to more closely resemble the product they hoped to eventually sell. They turned to their VC investors for advice. VC investors hope for the companies they invest in to attract more investors who are willing to pay a higher price than they themselves did for a company's stock. This raises the value of stock held by the original investors, bringing them closer to the ultimate goal of any VC: making a profitable "exit" by selling their shares through acquisitions or on the stock market as part of a public offering. With this in mind, and as Junyi's company was running out of time, Junyi's investors referred them to some potential investors and clients.

One of these potential clients was a "tech giant" – one of the biggest technology companies in the world. Junyi secured a meeting with the head of the company's VC arm, Ben, who was intrigued at the kind of robot that Junyi's team were trying to engineer. He invited them to "demo" a unit at their corporate campus at an agreed date and time. Ben specified what the unit ought to be able to do at that point: effectively clear debris, sort out different types of rubbish, operate via remote control, avoid obstacles, and cope with uneven ground and steps. Excited by the prospect of being able to work with a globally renowned company, Junyi eagerly ("拍心口") said yes.

The truth was that Junyi's team had no idea whether this was something they could achieve before meeting with Ben. Nonetheless, Junyi immediately got to work. He was also meeting other prospective clients at the same time. Many of these clients were inundated with requests to "demo" products from fledgling companies hoping to score a big contract, but they agreed to meet with Junyi because of his investors, whose global reputation and local ties with domestic governments signaled that Junyi should also be reliable (靠谱). Although they had agreed to meet, they were unsure about actually working with Junyi until they heard about the "tech giant's" interest in Junyi's robot. At that point, Junyi could not yet secure contracts with these potential clients, but he did manage to extract "letters of intent" from these meetings. These stated that, should Junyi secure expressed intent from the "tech giant" to use Junyi's robots, these clients would also be willing to use them too. As such, leveraging their investors' credibility, and the fame of the "tech giant," Junyi managed to establish a number of conditional, "weak" ties (Granovetter 1973).

As the date of the "demo" drew near, Junyi's team hit a snag in developing their new prototype. "It was exactly what they say. It is not the big things but the little things that kill you," he mused. We recalled how an up-and-coming "eco-conscious" fashion startup we both knew almost collapsed recently. Having overcome the arduous challenges of figuring out how to manufacture textiles from all sorts of recycled materials, they were held up by the humble zipper – their supplier was paralyzed by the pandemic. Even with the rest of their supply chain completely intact, the company did not have products they could sell, putting them financially deep "in the red." Junyi shook his head: "Even the great Achilles died of a mere arrow to his heel," he said.

Junyi's own Achilles heel was signal interference. Having engineered the rest of his robot to a satisfactory standard, Junyi's team was stumped by a problem with remote controlling the robot. The robot included a GPS sensor and a Wi-Fi receiver, which was necessary for the robot and its user to know its location, as well as for the user to control the robot remotely. For some reason, the signals seemed to interfere with each other and Junyi's team couldn't figure out why. They were so frustrated that they were reduced to what Junyi called "primitive behavior" — whacking the robot in exasperation. Adding further to their bewilderment was that, "for some reason, it sometimes worked!"

Junyi's startup spent more and more money on the problem, buying different models of the components to see if they could resolve the issue. By doing so, he dramatically accelerated their "burn rate." At one point, to counter the surging costs, he offered the whole office unpaid vacation time. "I told them that I know that we were all exhausted ("大家辛苦了"), that we all needed the time off. But the truth is, the company's funds were drying up."

On the actual day of the demo, Junyi and his team brought the robot to the campus. They had not resolved the issue, and they did not know what to do. It was just past lunch time, and, knowing that there was a demo scheduled for that day, the "tech giant's" employees began to stream out of the canteen and crowd around Junyi's team. As Junyi and his engineers fiddled with the unit, Junyi caught Ben's face in the crowd. Junyi recalled sweat dripping from his brow as he and one of his engineers stared at each other in utter panic. As a last resort, they huddled around the robot, shielding it from view. The engineer gave it a hearty thump. Miraculously, this worked: the robot operated perfectly for the few minutes of the demo. By the time the crowd started applauding, Junyi could no longer see Ben in the sea of faces. And when the team tried to restart the robot again, it no longer functioned. Junyi had never been religious, but for the miracle of those short few minutes when the robot worked, he thanked every deity he could think of.

Shortly after, Junyi received a letter of intent from Ben stating, on behalf of the "tech giant," their willingness to station a number of their robots on their campus for an extended period of time. The letter also detailed that if the robots were able to fulfill a set of requirements within the stated timeline, they would be keen to make a larger order. The time to harness the "strength of weak ties" had come (Granovetter 1973). With this letter of intent, and all the other letters of intent that predicated on it, Junyi and his cofounder immediately started knocking on VC investors' doors. Given this "surge" in interested users (a proxy for "demand"), Junyi's team secured another round of VC funding. Not only did Junyi's company narrowly avoid implosion, it actually shot up in value, as investors were willing to pay more for his company's shares.

When Junyi retold his story to his investors and fellow founders, they would applaud his gambit, which paid off. To them, it was not only an instance of great luck, but also an artful display of "growth hacking" for his startup company. As with other forms of "hacking," they considered it to be a craft in which virtuosic displays of craftiness in pursuit of justifiable ends were worthy of celebration (Coleman 2014, 2012). Even though Junyi was not technologically capable of producing the robot with the specifications that he promised on the day of the demo, to the community of investors and founders he belonged to, Junyi was not a con man. He was artfully managing social relationships to strategically postpone the day he would become technologically accountable, pushing it toward the horizon of an imminent yet unknown future.

Wabuwabu and Venture Capitalism

VC investors and startup founders inhabit what Guyer describes as "punctuated time," consisting of "fateful moments and turning points, the date as event rather than as position in a sequence or a cycle, dates as qualitatively different rather than quantitatively cumulative" (Guyer 2007, 416). Within "event-driven" time frames, these actors strategize to create and maintain configurations of ties that they can leverage to activate certain events, thus achieving what they call "scaling" or "acceleration."

There are parallels between what we observe here and what Reo Fortune describes as a "sharp trade practice" among the Dobu Islanders in Papua New Guinea. Fortune illustrates this practice – *wabuwabu* – through the account of one trader:

> Suppose I, Kisian of Tewara go [north] to the Trobriands and secure a [famous, prestigious] arm-shell called Monitor Lizard. Then I go [south] to Sanaroa and in four different places secure four different armshells promising each man who gives me a shell necklace Monitor Lizard in return, later. I, Kisian, do not have to be very specific in my promise. It will be conveyed by implication and assumption for the most part. Later, when four men appear at my home at Tewara, each expecting Monitor Lizard, only one will get it. The other three are not defrauded permanently however. They are furious, it is true, and their exchange is blocked for a year. Next year, when I, Kisian, go again to the Trobriands, I shall represent that I have four necklaces at home waiting for those who will give me four armshells. I obtain more armshells than I did previously, and pay my debts a year later... I have become a great man by enlarging my exchanges at the expense of blocking [the exchanges of others] for a year. I cannot afford to block their exchanges for too long, or my exchanges will never be trusted again. I am honest in the final issue (Fortune 1932, 515–20).

Kisian's demonstration of a "technical mastery of time" (Gell 2000, 262) puts the temporal technique I have described among Chinese startup entrepreneurs into stark sociohistorical relief: these temporal strategies are not new or unique to the tech industry or venture capitalism, nor are they inherently tied to the digital technologies they are used to foster.

VC folklore bears this out. One day over lunch during my fieldwork, I listened on as startup founders shared tales of their recent (mis)adventures in "sharp" temporal practices. One, who had come to Shenzhen from America, commented that this reminded him of a chain email he received as a teenager. It goes something like this:

A father tells his son to marry a girl of his choice. The son refuses, but the father tells him that the girl is Bill Gates' daughter. Hearing this, the son says, "in that case, okay!" The father then goes to Bill Gates and tells him that he wants Bill Gates' daughter to marry his son. Bill Gates initially rejects him, but the father tells him that his son is the CEO of the world's largest bank. Hearing this, Bill Gates says, "in that case, okay!" The father then goes to the president of the world's largest bank and tells him to appoint his son as the CEO of the bank. The president says no, but the father tells him that his son is the son-in-law of Bill Gates. Hearing this, the president says, "in that case, okay!"

"The email ends with 'And that's how you do business,'" the founder said. Everybody at the table laughed, recognizing themselves in the joke.

As this chain email and Fortune's documentation of the "sharp trade practices" among the Dobu suggest, these strategies of temporal "hacking" are not new. A key ingredient in Junyi's successful execution of this temporal strategy was the way he was initially able to leverage his investors' reputation and credibility. Guanxi, as a social resource, is among the critical resources that startup companies must leverage to keep up with the "gyroscopic" temporal rhythm (Xiang 2020) that participation in the VC model requires. His investors' constant cultivation and costly maintenance of guanxi relations thus paid off. Although it might be easy to mistake the role of the investor as merely providing funds, the social labor that VCs put in to propel the growth of the startup companies in their investment portfolios, while indirect, should not be overlooked.

This example shows how Junyi's startup company weaved social and financial leveraging practices together to avoid collapse and grow its valuation simultaneously. These insights into leveraging practices as one cog in the larger machinery of his business, reveal that beneath the sheen of novelty and hype, the VC model is underpinned by old sociotemporal strategies now rebranded as "growth hacking." As such, this chapter offers a reminder that critical scrutiny of the technological dimensions of startup growth should not come at the expense of attention to their embeddedness in sociocultural processes. The VC industry itself perpetuates the rhetoric of technological determinism that can mask the key social tools it employs, but anthropology is uniquely positioned to describe those tools and their vast and growing effects on the global (re)distribution of wealth and risk (cf. Miller 1998, 210).

CHAPTER 7

Entrepreneurship: A Dialogue with 2021 Symposium Authors

PATRICIA SUNDERLAND, ATAK AYAZ, RIDDHI BHANDARI, MATTHEW HILL, and JAMIE WONG

At the 2021 Entrepreneurship Symposium, rather than paper presentations, authors participated in a question-and-answer session moderated by Patricia Sunderland. Each author was asked a specific question, followed by questions that were posed to two of the four authors, and finally a question for all four authors. These questions and answers provide another filter to think about the authors' analyses as well as connections among them.

Sunderland: Question for Riddhi Bhandari

You have detailed the experiences and work journeys of small-scale tourism entrepreneurs in Agra, India, noting both the ruptures and continuities that are evident—even amidst the significant rupture, in fact shutdown, of tourism that accompanied the Covid-19 pandemic. Can you speak about some of the meanings, sentiments, and practicalities that have framed these tourism entrepreneurs' journeys both into and out of tourism and entrepreneurship?

Response: Riddhi Bhandari

Broadly speaking, Agra's tourism entrepreneurs' responses to the pandemic can be classified into two: the immediate search for alternatives that ranged from economic diversification to exploring politics as a site of entrepreneurship and the concurrent anxieties of feeling stuck, unable to move out of tourism, and a persisting sense of uncertainty. These responses are typical to Agra's entrepreneurs and capture the essence of how they consider tourism, as simultaneously risky and a source of opportunities, and how they approach risks—anxious and preoccupied with how to mitigate them while at the same time valorizing and romanticizing tourism's riskiness and their own risk-taking abilities.

Having worked in Agra since 2012, I have always struggled to reconcile this seemingly paradoxical approach through the entirety of my fieldwork but have slowly come to understand it as the ethic of entrepreneurialism in post-liberalized India that is shaped on the one hand by structures of work—entrepreneurs are resigned to the fact that there no longer exist desirable forms of work that are secure, certain and risk-free—and on the other by expectations of an entrepreneurial self that is measured and consolidated through one's willingness to engage with risks, to find strategies to work around them, and to be constantly on the lookout for alternatives.

This entrepreneurial affect informs entrepreneurs' everyday economic conduct in tourism and is also evident in entrepreneurs' responses to the pandemic as they journeyed, or at least made plans to journey, in and out of tourism.

Sunderland: Question for Atak Ayaz

You have made the point that the Turkish wine production that you studied was an example of "postindustrial" entrepreneurship and you have likened aspects of it as akin to the Vermont artisanal cheese producers that Heather Paxson (2013) has written about. Can you please give us an overview of some of the qualities of "post-industrial" production as you see it, illustrated with some examples taken from the Turkish wine entrepreneurs you worked with as well as other relevant examples.

Response: Atak Ayaz

This has been one of my guiding questions throughout as I attempt to differentiate industrial producers from postindustrial ones. I have three main points that I will highlight in my answer. First of all, postindustrial producers, in contrast to industrial producers, approach wine holistically. In the end, what they focus on is not only the bottle itself but how this wine bottle comes into being. They mostly start their journey by cultivating grapes rather than outsourcing from other vignerons. For this, they choose varieties that they want to process in their wineries and decide what kind of product they want to have at the end. This holistic approach enables postindustrial producers to observe and control their production, but this process of observation is not done to standardize production but rather to bring different tastes and characteristics of grape varieties and topographies to the final product. For example, almost all my interlocuters started by establishing their vineyards before the wineries, given that it takes three to five years for a grapevine to develop its fruit.

The second thing that separates industrial from postindustrial production is the economies of scale. Economies of scale are crucial for my discussion because my interlocuters are not aiming to produce in large quantities. With their small-scale production, they want to highlight the distinctive characters of their bottles, the distinctive characters of their soil, and the distinct characters of their production methodologies. To this end, grape cultivation and winemaking methods have also changed with postindustrial production in Turkey. Green pruning that decreases the total yield while increasing the grapes' phenolic quality is one example. Harvest time is another that depends on the taste of the grape, the winemakers with whom they collaborate, and changes depending on the grape varietals they use and the wine training implemented in their vineyards.

Lastly, the role of human and non-human actors in the winemaking process is an important topic. Postindustrial wine production brought the idea of terroir to the discussion. This made the location of production and soil qualities significant. Also, experts who take part in the production process became crucial. There is a term, "flying winemakers," for experts who travel from one part of the world to help producers and teach winery owners how to produce wine that they want. At the same time, the use of certain materials has begun to shift in this process. We began to talk about the role of the yeast, oak barrels, and other materials in determining and constructing taste. In all these ways, the idea of quality and taste have changed with the idea of post-industrialism.

Sunderland Question for Bhandari and Ayaz: Entrepreneurism and the State

For some of you, for instance Riddhi, governmental or state actions were seen and understood, including by entrepreneurs, as a crucial factor in the short and long term "health" and practicalities surrounding entrepreneurship. In Atak's work, the actions of the state (and tourism) were also mentioned. Can each of you talk about ways that you have seen the regulations, policies, desires, and actions of the state interacted and intersected with entrepreneurship? Crucially, as well, what are the desires of the entrepreneurs with whom you worked in terms of state intervention and support of entrepreneurship?

Response: Bhandari

Throughout my work with Agra's tourism entrepreneurs, I have been struck by their consistent effort to name and recognize the state (both as a unified monolith, Sarkar, as well as disaggregated into various governmental agencies engaged directly or indirectly in regulating tourism) as a critical economic actor whose actions and inactions define the scope and limits of entrepreneurialism and shape entrepreneurs' everyday economic conduct. In doing so, entrepreneurs' attempts can be considered as a critique of economic-liberalization ethos and policies, following which, the Indian state has looked to steadily withdraw from the economic sphere in favor of market forces but in practice has reconfigured its role as an economic beneficiary and market regulator without what entrepreneurs consider to be due responsibilities toward supporting and sustaining them.

Following the pandemic's economic fallout too, entrepreneurs continued to see beyond the public health crisis and the assumed inevitability of economic precarity to emphasize what the state could have done and can do to alleviate their precarity. Again, in keeping with the theme of continuities, many of these suggested measures transcended the specificity of the pandemic. In this vein, short-term and pandemic-specific recommendations included waiving taxes and utilities bills, providing medical insurance, and universal cash transfers to keep the economic wheel turning. For the long term, entrepreneurs expressed their desires that the state create sustainable tourism in Agra and reiterated the need for inclusive and community-informed policies that emerged in conversations with residents and entrepreneurs. Similarly, entrepreneurs expressed their desire that the state take more proactive steps to encourage local tourism and support local enterprise and entrepreneurs; currently, the popular perception is that the state supported big and "outside" businesses in favor of local ones. Some long-term measures that could engender sustainable, community-centered tourism include checking air and water pollution in Agra (seen as a deterrent to tourists), having an international airport closer to the city to decrease its dependence on Delhi, and developing a "tourism promenade" to connect key tourism sites and lined with shops, some of which ought to be reserved for local entrepreneurs.

Response: Ayaz

The role of the state is crucial to understand how quality enters this process. For this, there are two time periods that I specifically look at in my work. The first is the privatization of the state monopoly, TEKEL, which happened in 2004. Until that time, Turkey had a state monopoly controlling alcohol production. However, wine was not a part of it. Wine has been produced in today's Turkey since at least the Ottoman period. Today's Turkey has been accepted as one of the birthplaces of wine grapes, so grape cultivation has been one of the main activities of agrarian history in the region. Even though the state-owned production houses were the leading actor, making millions of liters of wine, other entrepreneurs were free to invest their money into winemaking since the Turkish Republic's foundation in 1923. In 2004, the current government (AKP-Justice and Development Party) privatized the state monopoly as a sign of the liberalization of the Turkish economy. However, there was a group of vignerons, mostly villagers, only producing grapes and selling them to state-owned facilities. With the privatization of the state monopoly, as the grape market became fully privatized, the unit price was primarily determined by private wineries and there was a little room for vignerons to negotiate. In the end, a significant number of vignerons stopped cultivating grapes and uprooted their vines. As a result, in 2008 only three percent of the grape cultivation in Turkey was used for wine. The political economy of grape cultivation is worth questioning to understand the changing pattern of winemaking in Turkey.

The second period begins with the enactment of the current law regulating alcohol sales and alcohol-related advertisement and sponsorship. The law was passed in 2013 when all these post-industrial entrepreneurs put their money into grape cultivation and winemaking. The law stipulates, "regardless of its form, advertisement and promotion for consumers cannot be carried out. Campaigns, promotions, and activities encouraging and promoting use and sale of these products cannot be organized. Only specialized fairs, academic publishing, and activities toward advertising alcoholic beverages on the international level can be organized." The privatization of TEKEL is one of the main reasons why these postindustrial wine owners shifted their capital to grape cultivation and winemaking in Turkey as there was an opening in the wine market. Even so, the 2013 law regulating the sale and promotion posed a major setback for postindustrial producers' entrepreneurial plans. So, they had to come up with new strategies to circumvent all these legalities. The oenotourism and wine routes on which my research focuses are the outcome of all this state control and manipulation.

Regarding the desires of the entrepreneurs with whom I worked… The taxes on alcohol are high in Turkey; it is one of the things that was frequently mentioned throughout my fieldwork. My interlocutors repeatedly stated that Turkey's wine industry would have achieved greater international recognition if the state supported the production.

Sunderland: Question for Jamie Wong

In your analysis focused on tech startups and venture capital (VC) in China, you have argued that venture capital investors assist startups by allowing them to "buy time." As you maintain, venture capitalists are ultimately "merchants of time" and you argue that there are parallels with these startup/venture capital practices and the "sharp trade practice" that Reo Fortune (1932) documented among the Dobu. Can you please elaborate on your notion of "temporal capital," and how it operates among tech startups and venture capital as well as the comparisons you see with Fortune's analysis.

Response: Jamie Wong

When I first encountered VC investors talking about "buying" time, I had thought that they were referring to a way to use money to somehow suspend or delay time. And that can be the case. In the course of my fieldwork, I have seen many instances where VC investors' injection of money was able to extend the life of a startup company on the verge of collapse. Eventually, however, I realized that what was going on was more complex than simply using money to buy time. VC investment and startup businesses are risky and precarious. As I spent more time with them, I saw that throwing money at problems can only be a partial solution—if it were a complete one, we would expect a direct correlation between the size of a VC fund and their returns-on-investment. However, this isn't the case.

What I hope to show instead is that the primary way VCs and startup founders are able to "manipulate time" is fundamentally social.

Whether to "buy" time, or to "accelerate" growth, these actors are in effect working to relax the constraints of temporal conventions—on themselves and the companies they invest in; and that, for the most part, is predicated on intertwined, laboriously maintained networks of trust.

In my dissertation, I show how VC firms spend time and resources to maintain precarious ties with Chinese local governments, which signals to domestic actors that they are politically sanctioned to work with and lends them credibility. This has cascading effects. We see that the VC firm's laboriously maintained credibility in turn lends credibility to the startup companies in which they have made investements. My paper argues, we are able to see that it is through this indirect and inferred vouching or "endorsement" ("背书" beishu) by the VC firm that Junyi's startup company can go on to make more provisional arrangements with business partners they would otherwise have no access to. And the more of these connections they make, they more they appear to be credible. The arrangements Junyi make with these business contacts are simultaneous and conditional on each other, and we see that by narrowly fulfilling the conditions of a big business contact, Junyi was able to leverage the provisional arrangements with multiple business partners to attract more investment into his company and achieve higher valuation.

This was a risky temporal play, but the way that these VCs and startup founders borrow and lend credibility and skillfully assemble a configuration of provisional arrangements that they can leverage has become conventionalized in VC circles. I call this practice "an art of scaling." In anthropology, we have mobilized concept-metaphors of expanding factory production (Geertz 1963) or magnifying digital reproduction (Tsing 2012) to invoke and analyze the notion of "scaling." I am trying to show here that "scaling" can take a very different form. Among VC investors and early-stage startup companies, "scaling" resembles instead the scaling of boulders—whereby points of contact momentarily serve to leverage the climber upward.

Although I have mentioned that we have seen no direct correlation between the initial size of a VC fund and their returns-on-investment, it is the case that VC funds that do well appear to do better and better. Why is that? This is where the notion of "temporal capital" comes in.

I am of course drawing heavily on Bourdieu to develop this notion. And what I am trying to highlight here are issues of conversion, accumulation, and inequality. We know from existing anthropological scholarship that in China, guanxi (or relations) is a form of social capital, that guanxi begets more guanxi. In this way, they also resemble what Guyer and Belinga discuss as "wealth in people" in Cameroon—whereby social power, knowledge, and status are achieved, mediated, maintained, and accrued through social ties, affiliations, and dependents (1995).

In my fieldwork I have seen that the ability to use "temporal hacks" or what Ringel might call strategies of "time-tricking" (2016) is predicated on social relations or guanxi. As Bourdieu has discussed, there is a degree of convertibility between different capitals (e.g., social, cultural, economic) (2018). Since we know well that "wealth in people" can be accumulated, I am highlighting through my work that the ability to navigate and manipulate social time—or temporal agency—can also be accumulated, like a kind of "temporal capital."

In *Forms of Capital*, Bourdieu discusses how social capital, or any other form of capital really, is a mechanism of generational reproduction of inequality (2018). This generational element resonates with my fieldwork in China, where VC investors are vernacularly called "Daddy Moneybags" (金主爸爸). Moreover, we have seen that investors' credibility and temporal capital have implications for their dependents —the startups they invest in; that there is a degree of inheritance of temporal capital. Given this, I think my work prompts us to ask: What is the criteria and logics of inclusion or exclusion to temporal capital? What are the mechanisms of inheritance? For whom are these temporal hacks or techniques sanctioned? What is the extent and quality of the consequences of inequality as a result of this divide?

Sunderland: Question for Matthew Hill

In your paper, you maintain that in light of the Covid-19 pandemic, the pseudonymous "Major Metropolitan Credit Union" (MMCU) was committed to 'adapt', or as the VP put it, 'adjust to our new normal'—remote work, digital processes, growing demand for mobile and online services—without losing touch with its cooperative values." Moreover, you note that you see the process of digital transformation as a form of cooperative entrepreneurialism as formulated by Bolton et al (2019) regarding cheese in rural Peru. Could you please elaborate on the concept of cooperative entrepreneurialism, talking about the conceptual underpinnings of "cooperative entrepreneurialism" and how you see it playing out—in your own as well as other settings.

Response: Matthew Hill

I use the term "cooperative entrepreneurialism" to refer to credit unions' status as not-for-profit, member-owned, "cooperative associations" that exist to "underwrite loans" to members and "stabilize and ameliorate" their financial lives (Nelms and Rea 2019:7). Such credit cooperatives were started to create savings and thrift organizations for workers not served by commercial banking institutions in early 1900s. In 1934, Congress passed the Federal Credit Union Law of 1934, allowing credit unions to incorporate in any U.S. state or territory, and strengthened the relationship between the credit union system and the federal banking system.

My paper raises the question of how MMCU will maintain this cooperative ethos as it transitions from an "older cooperative model" based on personal, face-to-face branch interactions to a "new cooperative model" that constitutes community in digital and virtual channels (Nelms & Rea 2019:9). The challenge for MMCU is to carve out an alternative market segment that will allow it to compete with commercial banks and fintech startups without losing touch with its collectivist values.

In terms of cooperative entrepreneurialism, the question is what do we mean by "entrepreneurship" and on what aspect of it do we focus (markets, organizations, networks, behaviors)? Schumpter (1934) defined (private) entrepreneurialism in terms of "innovation and change agency." The function of the entrepreneur is to "reform or revolutionize the pattern of production, by exploiting an invention, or untried technological possibility for producing a new commodity or an old one in new ways" (Clamp and Alhamis 2010:152). Entrepreneurship, then, is seen as a rational response to competitive pressures to generate profits for individuals or organizations.

Social or civic entrepreneurship is focused on creating social benefits, where firms and individuals become more responsive/responsible to their communities, playing a role in civic regeneration in disadvantaged communities. An example would be setting up a community computing facility to help local residents develop IT skills.

Cooperative entrepreneurialism is more self-help economic activity focused on serving the members of the cooperative. Depending on the mission of the cooperative, it may or may not be linked to building the local economy. For MMCU, the issue of cooperative entrepreneurialism is whether MMCU will be able to leverage new digital technologies like Artficial Intelligence/Machine Learning (AI/ML), cloud, internet of things, blockchain, predictive analytics, to better serve existing members, and to attract new members to the cooperative, without losing touch with its cooperative values. It hinges on whether the credit union can move beyond merely moving its existing products and services online to actually transforming its business and customer experience. In the paper, I give the example of a university credit union in Los Angeles that used AI driven bots to manage 75 percent of call center calls and sent call center employees to a two-year financial planning program at UCLA so they could help members with financial planning. Another example involves a credit union that created a data warehouse to identify members who might be going through financial stress or have opportunities to refinance mortgages.

Sunderland Question for Wong and Hill: Converging and Competing Interests

It can certainly be argued that for entrepreneurship—as well as capitalism and social life more generally – dynamics of converging and competing interests are often key. It seems to me that in the case of tech startups and venture capital as described by Jamie Wong and the journey of digital change in a metropolitan credit union as described by Matthew Hill, the interplay of converging and competing interests were crucial to ongoing social action as well as outcomes. Can you please discuss how you and the people you worked with saw and analyzed converging and competing interests as a crucial aspect of their social world and entrepreneurship?

Response: Wong

In the early days of my fieldwork, one of the most striking things to me was how there is no illusion among any of my VC interlocutors that the price or valuation of startup companies resemble any notion of an economic "equilibrium," or that this is all part of self-balancing market.

These VC investors were the "market forces," so to speak. Startup companies are by definition in earlier stages, and not listed on stock markets or traded on public exchanges. The group of investors with the access to invest in these startups are small, and to further consider what is locally called goutongchengben (沟通成本; communication cost) or what would be "imperfect information" in economic parlance, the amount of VC investors each startup can reach is even smaller. In a volume edited by MacKenzie, Muniesa, and Siu, scholars have explored how markets are performatively "made" (2008). In like manner, my VC and startup interlocutors are actively making markets in their day-to-day work. And in this making of markets, the interplay of converging and competing interests are crucial—because in the domain of early-stage companies that is venture capitalism, competing interests are converging interests.

For example: When I entered the field in China in 2018, many startups have sprung up to offer medical diagnostic services, and they were in demand. However, this coincided with the implosion of Theranos, the infamous biotech startup founded by Elizabeth Holmes, which was exposed for massive fraud and deception of their investors. One investor I knew in Beijing, who I will call Zhang, had backed a domestic diagnostics startup company. Before the Theranos scandal, this investor had every intention to follow-up his investment in the domestic biotech startup company I mentioned—to keep supporting their research and development by giving them more funds, and to increase his firm's stake in the startup. However, other VC investors began to fret about being defrauded after the Theranos scandal. Though Zhang still firmly believed this startup company had something meaningful to offer to society, he was not confident that other VC investors would recover from this scare quickly enough to compete and try to outbid him and other investors for the startup company's shares in the foreseeable future. If they don't, his shares would ultimately be worthless. VC investors are managers of funds and face their own deadlines from their own investors at the end of their funds' lifespans. If Zhang can't sell his shares in the biotech startup at a profit by the end of the fund in a few years' time, they would in effect be worthless. For this reason, he decided that the money he invested in the company was sunk cost, and not to follow up on his investment. This rendition is somewhat simplified, but this is what I mean when I say competing interests are converging interests. For capitalistic models to work at all, there has to be competition, someone has to be excluded, and this is just more apparent in these early-stage markets, where the social nature of these economic activities is more plainly in sight.

Response: Hill

The converging and competing interests centered around the adoption of and resistance to new forms of digital/virtual community and association. MMCU's "cooperative idea" of entrepreneurship is based on the past 100 years of credit union history (following the Federal Credit Union Act of 1934) in which members formed "cooperative associations" using their deposits to underwrite loans to fellow co-op members (Nelms and Rea 2019:7). This basis creates a strong sense of place-based attachment and in the case of MMCU, there is a strong sense of belonging based on a mortgage discount program, sponsorship of school programs, and efforts to make the workplace fun and engaging through happy hours and tailgate parties. MMCU employees strongly identify with the cooperative aspect, emphasizing that they are not a bank and that they exist to serve their members.

Even in the light of the pandemic, which commercial banks used as an opportunity to slash jobs and close branches, MMCU provided generous paid time off and remote work options to its employees, opened a new branch, and assisted financially stressed members with auto and home loans through a generous skip-a-pay program. MMCU's leadership also resisted the pandemic-induced shift to remote work by issuing a series of 90-day return to work plans in the summer of 2020 that in conjunction with safety measures such as touchless toilets, plexiglass barriers, and directional arrows at headquarters were intended to recreate the old face-to-face family culture. The leadership was also slow to embrace the hiring of remote IT talent from outside of its metropolitan region to help it implement the financial technologies and backend platforms required for digital transformation as it was also associated with the loss of MMCU jobs.

Yet, technological innovations have changed the way in which credit unions interact with their members and are disrupting the place-based definition of membership and community that have defined credit unions over the past century. As work becomes increasingly mobile, the types of workplace and geographic associations that defined a sense of community in credit unions is becoming increasingly frayed. Similarly, with the shift to mobile and online banking, the basis of communal, common bonds is also being disrupted. Covid-19 accelerated these trends at MMCU, as employees became accustomed to working remotely, and members turned to mobile channels over branch transactions. For MMCU, this meant noving financial services online with increased digital engagement in payments and mobile app engagement. It was a crash course in digital transformation, remote notarization, deposit, bill pay, money transfer, P2P payments, digital loan application processing, and video conferencing. Digital account opening, onboarding, digital credit scoring, underwriting through increased use of chatbots, identity solutions, advance analytics with solid data management and governance were all part of the process. There were also growing opportunities for fintech of Credit Union Service Organization partnerships as well as the consolidation and repurposing of branches and branch staff.

Sunderland Question for All: Implication of Methods and Approach

Could each of you speak briefly about the methods and approach you used in your field-work and contemplate how your method and approach affected your findings and realizations? Please also comment on how you see your findings and realizations as distinct from what others have analyzed vis-à-vis entrepreneurship, whether these others are anthropologists or from other fields.

Response: Bhandari

Contrary to many scholars who found their research disrupted with the pandemic and had to quickly adopt and adapt to new digital research methods, digital interactions were already a longstanding part of the communication between me and my research participants, much before I began this specific leg of research.

I have been working with Agra's tourism entrepreneurs since 2012, and the digital has always been an important medium in our interactions; even when I was in Agra, I befriended many of them on Instagram (I am not on Facebook although that is the preferred social media platform for most). WhatsApp has been a consistent medium, solidifying its centrality as I moved away from Agra. There are the generic good morning messages as well as specific messages about life events and politics. Occasionally, someone calls me or I call them to catch up with one another. My method (of digital ethnography) preceded and even determined the specific research question or topic: When the pandemic started, I was in regular touch with many entrepreneurs in Agra as we tried to keep track of our and our family's health and well-being.

The novelty for me was the insights that this particular leg of the research offered for approaching markets and entrepreneurs. Typically, research in markets and with entrepreneurs is, for lack of a better word, centered around action: there is constant movement of people, goods, things that one needs to keep track of and I recall being on my feet and on the move, engaged in peripatetic fieldwork as I worked with and tried to keep up with Agra's tourism entrepreneurs. This attention to action emphasizes and reinforces one's understanding of entrepreneurialism as the individual-centered, hero-narrative of innovation and creative destruction.

However, this time and with the pandemic, there was a stillness, a "stuckness" if one can call it that: entrepreneurs were stuck, unable to work or find work (even when the markets opened, tourists failed to show). Consequently, the action of entrepreneurialism was trumped by conversations heavy with entrepreneurs' anxieties, aspirations, the thought processes of what next and the waiting and watching for things to return to movement.

I think re-centering the still and the affective aspects of entrepreneurialism can further enhance the theoretical field because they emphasize the structures of work and the role of the state, both current and futuristically hopeful, within which individual entrepreneurial actions are situated, and that define the contours of entrepreneurialism.

Response: Ayaz

Throughout my research, I made use of the fact that I am from Turkey and my research focuses on the country. Before my fieldwork began, whenever I flew back to Turkey from Switzerland, I took a trip to visit post-industrial wineries on the Thracian wine route. To better understand how winemakers and winery owners cast meaning for business, sentiments, and agricultural entrepreneurialism and how they construct their narratives, I conducted semi-structured interviews and follow-ups. In one of those initial interviews, I posed a very general question to a winery owner: "How did you decide to establish a winery?" He leaned back on his big chair, crossed his arms, and immediately began to answer my question with his pre-set wordings: "I started by asking myself this question…." In most of the wineries, one of the first things that grabbed my attention was clippings from newspapers or magazines framed and put on the wall. These pieces indicate that winery owners/investors have often already given several interviews to (inter)national journalists.

As an anthropologist, to go beyond these readymade answers and learn more about how they connect with grapes and wine bottles, I decided to invest my time and energy to work as a cellar worker in post-industrial wineries. In doing so, I developed closer relations with my interlocutors and had more time to conduct participant observation. Actively working in a winery brought many benefits to my research. Spending a significant amount of time with winemakers and other cellar workers helped inform me immensely about gatherings the other winemakers had: for example, the meetings of the wine route that I was studying and the wine tastings done in other institutions. Thus, I had the chance to attend the exclusive meetings of other winemakers, winery owners, and state workers. By investing my physical labor into my research, I developed deeper relations with my interlocutors. Moreover, it helped me understand how legal documents are in movement within these wineries and how they deal with different regulations coming from the state.

Response: Wong

My first entry in to my field site was through a joint program between a Chinese and a U.S. university that introduces student and alumni startups to local businesses. It gave me access to investors, to startups, and their business and government partners. I attended a lot of meetings with them —meetings for startup pitches, for investors to scout startups, for partnership with governments, with other investors. Eventually, I based myself at a VC firm in Shenzhen to be a participant-observer. This field site includes an open office space for startups in which they have made an investment and now have partial ownership. Doing fieldwork there gave me a chance to observe both the investors and the startups' day-to-day operations.

So far on the panel, I have spoken a lot about credibility and precarity, and I think I am particularly attuned to these themes because doors were opened to me because of borrowed credibility through my association with MIT, Tsinghua, and eventually with this one particular VC firm, but the maintenance of access was never guaranteed. I was in these settings as a researcher from an American graduate school at a time when U.S.-China tensions were high.

Although the people who hosted me showed great hospitality, there was also no doubt that if at any point I became a liability, they would revoke my access. I was privy to business plans, government plans, and sensitive IP-protected information, the confidentiality of which is the basis of startup companies' survival. Unlike employees working for these funds and companies, for the sake of being able to publish my research, I did not sign an NDA. Nonetheless, the issue of an NDA was brought up repeatedly during the three years of my fieldwork, which meant that I had to constantly be alert that this was something that I might need to negotiate again.

Ultimately, what allowed me to complete my fieldwork was the trust that I built and maintained with my interlocutors. I actively learned from my interlocutors' approach to weave webs of borrowed credibility to expand my own network of people I could talk to and interview.

I think my work is different in the way it builds on existing work by tying together strands that were not previously brought together in this particular way. I connect the work on social ties in business and government by Osburg (2013) and Uretsky (2016), with anthropological discussions of temporal strategies such as those by Fortune (1932) and Bourdieu (1977). In doing so, I also build upon Bear's work on labor in/of time by showing how actors in my field adopt conventionalized techniques not only to survive and mediate temporal rhythms (2014b), but to hack and game them.

Response: Hill

My fieldwork with MMCU took place in the role of a consultant conducting applied research within organizations. In that role, I am part insider as well as outsider. It means documenting the culture, but also working to transform it together with the client. So, it means working with, not for, the client through collaborative research projects. In the case of MMCU it is a long-standing relationship that can last for many years. It is similar to traditional fieldwork in which you peel the layers of the onion and gain deeper insights over time.

The focus is on working both horizontally and vertically, improving processes but also larger strategies. It is about becoming part of the culture, but also remaining an outsider, so not becoming completely absorbed by the culture or situation. Rather, the goal is to reflect on the culture and bring others into that reflection and dialogue as well and thereby attempting to nudge the culture in new directions through collaborative research, identifying pain points, developing a shared point of view, and attempting small experiments in making change. It is about getting people to tell stories in their own words and allowing others to hear pains or frustrations so they can work collaboratively on finding shared solutions. In terms of fieldwork under Covid-19, this also meant taking part in many virtual townhalls.

References Cited

African Entrepreneurialsm: The Emergence of Ethiopian Gurage Entrepreneurs as a National Capitalist Class
Worku Nida

Aldrich, Howard, and Roger Waldinger.1990. "Ethnicity and Entrepreneurship." *Annual Review of Sociology* 16: 111-35. https://doi.org/10.1146/annurev.so.16.080190.000551

Ardener, Shirely, and Sandra Burman, eds. 1995. *Money Go Round: The Importance of Savings and Credit Associations for Women.* Oxford: Berg.

Aredo, Dejene. 1991."The Potentials of the Iqqub as an Indigenous Institution Financing Small- and Micro-scale Enterprises in Ethiopia." The Hague: Conference Paper.

Barth, Fredrik. 1962. *The Role of the Entrepreneur in Social Change in Northern Norway.* Bergen: Norwegian Universities Press.

Beresford, Melissa. 2020. "Entrepreneurship as Legacy Building: Reimagining the Economy in Post-Apartheid South Africa." *Economic Anthropology* 7: 65-79. https://doi.org/10.1002/sea2.12170

Bonacich, Edna. 1973. A Theory of Middleman Minorities. *American Sociological Review* 38: 583-94.

Bonacich, Edna and John Modell. 1981. *The Economic Basis of Ethnic Solidarity: A Study of Japanese Americans.* Berkeley and Los Angeles: University of California Press.

Bonsa, Shimelis. 1997. Migration, Urbanization and Urban Labor Undertakings: The Case of the Kistane of Addis Ababa, ca. 1900-1974. MA thesis, Addis Ababa University.

Buttler, John. S. 2005. *Entrepreneurship and Self-help among Black Americans.* Albany: State University of New York Press.

Central Statistical Authority (CSA). 1999. Ethiopia: Statistical Abstract 1998. Addis Ababa: Central Statistical Office Ethiopia.

Ferguson, James. 1994. *The Anti-Politics Machine: Development, Depoliticization, and Bureaucratic Power in Lesotho.* Minneapolis: University of Minnesota Press.

Geertz, Clifford. 1963. *Peddlers and Princes: Social Change and Economic Modernization in Two Indonesian Towns.* Chicago: University of Chicago Press.

Gupta, Akhil. 1994. *Indian Entrepreneurial Culture.* London: Wishwa Prakashan.

Hale, Sondra. 1979. "The Changing Ethnic Identity of Nubians in an Urban Milieu: Khartoum, Sudan." PhD dissertation, University of California, Los Angeles.

Hefner, Robert, ed. 1998. *Market Cultures: Society and Morality in the New Asian Capitalisms.* Boulder, CO: Westview Press.

Jalloh, Alusine. 1999. *African Entrepreneurship: Muslim Fula Merchants in Sierra Leone.* Athens: Ohio University Center for International Studies: Ohio University Press.

Light, Ivan., and Steven. Gold. 2000. *Ethnic Economies.* San Diego, CA: Academic Press.

Moyo, Dambisa. 2009. *Dead Aid: Why Aid Is Not Working and How There Is a Better Way for Africa.* New York: Farrar, Straus and Giroux.

Nida, Worku. 2006. *The Impacts of Urban Migration on Village Life: The Gurage Case.* Addis Ababa: Addis Ababa University Press.

Nida, Worku. 1996. "Gurage Urban Migration and the Dynamics of Cultural Life in the Village." In *Essays on Gurage Language and Culture,* edited by Grover Hudson. Wiesbaden: Harrassowitz Verlag.

Nida, Worku. 1993. "The *waq* Cult of the Gurage." In *Proceedings of the 11th International Conference on Ethiopian Studies.* Addis Ababa: Addis Ababa University Press

Nida, Worku. 1991. *Jabidu: YaGurage Hizb Bahilena Tarik* ('Jabidu: The Gurage culture and history'). Addis Ababa: Bole Printing Press.

Nida, Worku. 1990. "The traditional beliefs of the Gurage with particular emphasis on the *Bozha* cult," In *Proceedings of the 1st National Conference on Ethiopian Studies.* Addis Ababa: Addis Ababa University Press.

Pankhurst, Richard, and Andreas Eshete. 1956. "Self-help in Ethiopia." *Ethiopia Observer* 2 (2): 354-64.

Porters, Alejandro, and Robert Back. 1985. *Latin Journey: Cuban and Mexican immigrants in the United States.* Berkeley: University of California Press.

Rodney, Walter. 1983. *How Europe Underdeveloped Africa.* Washington, DC: Howard University Press.

Rutashobya, Lettice K. 1998. *Women Entrepreneurship in Tanzania: Entry and Performance Barriers.* Addis Ababa, Ethiopia: OSSREA (Organization for Social Science Research in Eastern and Southern Africa).

Shack, William. A. 1966. *The Gurage: A People of the ensete Culture.* London: Oxford University Press.

Shack, William A. 1976. "Urban Ethnicity and the Cultural Process of Urbanization in Ethiopia," In *Urban Anthropology: Cross-cultural Studies in Urbanization,* edited by Aidan Southall. Oxford: Oxford University Press.

Tarrow, Sidney. 1998. *Power in Movement: Social Movements and Contentious Politics.* Cambridge: Cambridge University Press.

Temtime, Zewedu. 1995. "A Social History of Arada c. 1890-1935: A Survey." MA thesis, Addis Ababa University.

Waldinger, Roger, Howard Aldrich, and Robin Ward. 1990. *Ethnic Entrepreneurs: Immigrant Business in Industrial Societies.* London: SAGE.

Weber, Max. [1904-05] 1992. *The Protestant Ethic and the Spirit of Capitalism.* New York: Routledge.

Zewde, Bahru. 1987. "Early Safars of Addis Ababa: Patterns of Evolution." In *Proceedings of the International Symposium on the Centenary of Addis Ababa,* edited by Ahmed Zekaria, Bahru Zewde, and Taddese Beyene. Addis Ababa: Institute of Ethiopian Studies, Addis Ababa University.

Of Sciences and Startups: An Anthropological Perspective on Academic Venturing
Lora Koycheva

Aldridge, T. Taylor, and David Audretsch. 2011. "The Bayh-Dole Act and Scientist Entrepreneurship." *Research Policy*, 40(8): 1058-67. https://doi.org/10.1016/j.respol.2011.04.006

Amabile, Teresa M., and Michael G. Pratt. 2016. "The Dynamic Componential Model of Creativity and Innovation in Organizations: Making Progress, Making Meaning." *Research in Organizational Behavior* 36: 157-83. https://doi.org/10.1016/j.riob.2016.10.001

Baker, Ted, and Reed E. Nelson. 2005. "Creating Something from Nothing: Resource Construction through Entrepreneurial Bricolage." *Administrative Science Quarterly* 50(3): 329-66. https://doi.org/10.2189/asqu.2005.50.3.329

Bathelt, Harald, and Ben Spigel. 2011. "University Spin-offs, Entrepreneurial Environment and Start-up Policy: The Cases of Waterloo and Toronto (Ontario) and Columbus (Ohio)." *International Journal of Knowledge-Based Development* 2(2): 202-19. https://doi.org/10.1504/IJKBD.2011.041248

Bergmann, Heiko, Christian Hundt, and Rolf Sternberg. 2016. "What Makes Student Entrepreneurs? On the Relevance (and Irrelevance) of the University and the Regional Context for Student Start-ups." *Small Business Economics* 47(1): 53-76. https://doi.org/10.1007/s11187-016-9700-6

Bourdieu, Pierre. *Homo Academicus.* Stanford University Press, 1988.

Bramwell, Allison, and David A. Wolfe. 2008. "Universities and Regional Economic Development: The Entrepreneurial University of Waterloo." *Research Policy* 37(8): 1175-87. https://doi.org/10.1016/j.respol.2008.04.016

Breugst, Nicola, and Rebecca Preller. 2020. "Where the Magic happens: Opening the Black Box of Entrepreneurial Team Functioning." In *The Psychology of Entrepreneurship*, edited by Michael M. Gielnik, Melissa S. Cardon, and Michael Frese, pp. 80-96. New York: Routledge.

Briody, Elizabeth K., and Alex Stewart. 2019. "Entrepreneurship: A Challenging, Fruitful Domain for Ethnography." *Journal of Business Anthropology* 8(2): 141-66.

Browder, Russell E., Howard E. Aldrich, and Steven W. Bradley. 2019. "The Emergence of the Maker Movement: Implications for Entrepreneurship Research." *Journal of Business Venturing* 34(3): 459-76. https://doi.org/10.1016/j.jbusvent.2019.01.005

Cardon, Melissa S., Joakim Wincent, Jagdip Singh, and Mateja Drnovsek. 2009. "The Nature and Experience of Entrepreneurial Passion." *Academy of Management Review* 34(3): 511-32. https://doi.org/10.5465/amr.2009.40633190

Clarysse, Bart, Mike Wright, Andy Lockett, Philippe Mustar, and Mirjam Knockaert. 2007. "Academic Spin-offs, Formal Technology Transfer and Capital Raising." *Industrial and Corporate Change* 16(4): 609-40. https://doi.org/10.1093/icc/dtm019

Coleman, E. Gabriella, and Alex Golub. 2008. "Hacker Practice: Moral Genres and the Cultural Articulation of Liberalism." *Anthropological Theory* 8(3): 255-77. https://doi.org/10.1177/1463499608093814

Colombo, Massimo, Philippe Mustar, and Mike Wright. 2010. "Dynamics of Science-Based Entrepreneurship." *Journal of Technology Transfer* 35(1): 1-15. https://doi.org/10.1007/s10961-009-9114-6

Colyvas, Jeannette A. 2007. "From Divergent Meanings to Common Practices: The Early Institutionalization of Technology Transfer in the Life Sciences at Stanford University." *Research Policy* 36(4): 456-76. https://doi.org/10.1016/j.respol.2007.02.019

Eisenhardt, Kathleen M. 1989. "Building Theories from Case Study Research." *Academy of Management Review* 14(4): 532-50. https://doi.org/10.5465/amr.1989.4308385

Etzkowitz, Henry. 1993. "Technology Transfer: The Second Academic Revolution." *Technology Access Report* 6(7): 7-9.

Etzkowitz, Henry, and Magnus Klofsten. 2005. "The Innovating Region: Toward a Theory of Knowledge-based Regional Development." *R&D Management* 35(3): 243-255. https://doi.org/10.1111/j.1467-9310.2005.00387.x

Fini, Riccardo, Rosa Grimaldi, Simone Santoni, and Maurizio Sobrero. 2011. "Complements or Substitutes? The Role of Universities and Local Context in Supporting the Creation of Academic Spin-offs." *Research Policy* 40(8): 1113-27. https://doi.org/10.1016/j.respol.2011.05.013

Fish, Jefferson M. 2000. "What Anthropology Can Do for Psychology: Facing Physics Envy, Ethnocentrism, and a Belief in 'Race.'" *American Anthropologist* 102(3): 552-63. https://www.jstor.org/stable/683411

Forbes, Daniel P. 2005. "The Effects of Strategic Decision Making on Entrepreneurial Self–efficacy." *Entrepreneurship Theory and Practice* 29(5): 599-626. https://doi.org/10.1111/j.1540-6520.2005.00100.x

Foster, Jacob G., Andrey Rzhetsky, and James A. Evans. 2015. "Tradition and Innovation in Scientists' Research Strategies." *American Sociological Review* 80(5): 875-908. https://doi.org/10.1177/0003122415601618

Gartner, William B. 1989. "Some Suggestions for Research on Entrepreneurial Traits and Characteristics." *Entrepreneurship Theory and Practice* 14(1): 27-38. https://doi.org/10.1177/104225878901400103

Geissler, Mario, Steffen Jahn, and Peter Haefner. 2010. "The Entrepreneurial Climate at Universities: The Impact of Organizational Factors." In *The Theory and Practice of Entrepreneurship*, edited by David Smallbone, João Leitão, Mário Raposo, and Friederike Welter. Cheltenham: Edward Elgar. https://doi.org/10.4337/9781849805933.00007

Gehman, Joel, Vern L. Glaser, Kathleen M. Eisenhardt, Denny Gioia, Ann Langley, and Kevin G. Corley. 2018. "Finding Theory–Method Fit: A Comparison of Three Qualitative Approaches to Theory Building." *Journal of Management Inquiry* 27(3): 284-300. https://doi.org/10.1177/1056492617706029

Greenfield, Patricia M. 2000. "What Psychology Can Do for Anthropology, or Why Anthropology Took Postmodernism on the Chin." *American Anthropologist* 102(3): 564-76. https://doi.org/10.1525/aa.2000.102.3.564

Grimaldi, Rosa, Martin Kenney, Donald S. Siegel, and Mike Wright. 2011. "30 Years after Bayh–Dole: Reassessing Academic Entrepreneurship." *Research Policy* 40(8): 1045-57. https://doi.org/10.1016/j.respol.2011.04.005

Guerrero, Maribel, David Urbano, James A. Cunningham, and Eduardo Gajón. 2018. "Determinants of Graduates' Start-ups Creation across a Multi-Campus Entrepreneurial University: The Case of Monterrey Institute of Technology and Higher Education." *Journal of Small Business Management* 56(1): 150-78. https://doi.org/10.1111/jsbm.12366

Hayter, Roger. 1997. *The Dynamics of Industrial Location: The Factory, the Firm and the Production System*. Hoboken, NJ: Wiley.

Hayter, Christopher S., Roman Lubynsky, and Spiro Maroulis. 2017. "Who Is the Academic Entrepreneur? The Role of Graduate Students in the Development of University Spinoffs." *Journal of Technology Transfer* 42(6): 1237-54. https://doi.org/10.1007/s10961-016-9470-y

Haeussler, Carolin, and Jeannette A. Colyvas. 2011. "Breaking the Ivory Tower: Academic Entrepreneurship in the Life Sciences in UK and Germany." *Research Policy* 40(1): 41-54. https://doi.org/10.1016/j.respol.2010.09.012

Hickman, Jacob R. 2010. "Psychology and Anthropology." In *21st Century Anthropology. A Reference Handbook,* edited by H. James Birx. Thousand Oaks, CA: SAGE, pp. 950-59.

Hmieleski, Keith M., and E. Erin Powell. 2018. "The Psychological Foundations of University Science Commercialization: A Review of the Literature and Directions for Future Research." *Academy of Management Perspectives* 32(1): 43-77. https://doi.org/10.5465/amp.2016.0139

Hollan, Douglas. 2005. "Setting a New Standard: The Person-centered Interviewing and Observation of Robert I. Levy." *Ethos* 33(4): 459-66. https://doi.org/10.1525/eth.2005.33.4.459

Huyghe, Annelore, Mirjam Knockaert, Evila Piva, and Mike Wright. 2016. "Are Researchers Deliberately Bypassing the Technology Transfer Office? An Analysis of TTO Awareness." *Small Business Economics* 47(3): 589-607. https://doi.org/10.1007/s11187-016-9757-2

Julien, Pierre-André. 2008. *A Theory of Local Entrepreneurship in the Knowledge Economy*. Chelthenham: Edward Elgar.

Klofsten, Magnus, Alain Fayolle, Maribel Guerrero, Sarfraz Mian, David Urbano, and Mike Wright. 2019. "The Entrepreneurial University as Driver for Economic Growth and Social Change-Key Strategic Challenges." *Technological Forecasting and Social Change* 141: 149-58. https://doi.org/10.1016/j.techfore.2018.12.004

Koycheva, Lora. 2019. "Prototyping the Entrepreneurial Self: Ethnographic Insights into Identity Transformation during Venture Creation in Makerspace Hackathons." G-Forum Annual Conference, Vienna, Austria.

Krabel, Stefan, and Pamela Mueller. 2009. "What Drives Scientists to Start Their Own Company?: An Empirical Investigation of Max Planck Society Scientists." *Research Policy* 38(6): 947-56. https://doi.org/10.1016/j.respol.2009.02.005

Levy, Robert I., and Douglas W. Hollan. 1998. "Person-Centered Interviewing and Observation." In *Handbook of Methods in Cultural Anthropology*, edited by H. Russell Bernard, pp. 333-64. Walnut Grove, CA: SAGE.

Lifshitz-Assaf, Hila, Sarah Lebovitz, and Lior Zalmanson. 2018. "The Importance of Breaking Instead of Compressing Time in Accelerated Innovation: A Study of Makeathons' New Product Development Process." *Available at SSRN 3280219.*

Marshall, H. J. 2018. "Once You Support, You Are Supported": Entrepreneurship and Reintegration Among Ex-Prisoners in Gulu, Northern Uganda. *Economic Anthropology,* 5(1): 71-82. https://doi.org/10.1002/sea2.12103

Morais, Robert J., and Timothy de Waal Malefyt. 2010. "How Anthropologists Can Succeed in Business: Mediating Multiple Worlds of Inquiry." *International Journal of Business Anthropology* 1(1): 45-56.

Moriano, Juan A., Marjan Gorgievski, Mariola Laguna, Ute Stephan, and Kiumars Zarafshani. 2012. "A Cross-Cultural Approach to Understanding Entrepreneurial Intention." *Journal of Career Development* 39(2): 162-85.

Müller, Ruth. 2014 "Postdoctoral Life Scientists and Supervision Work in the Contemporary University: A Case Study of Changes in the Cultural Norms of Science." *Minerva* 52(3): 329-49. https://doi.org/10.1007/s11024-014-9257-y

Nader, Laura. 2011. "Ethnography as Theory." *HAU: Journal of Ethnographic Theory* 1(1): 211-19. https://doi.org/10.14318/hau1.1.008

Niosi, Jorge. 2006. "Success Factors in Canadian Academic Spin-offs." *The Journal of Technology Transfer* 31(4): 451-57. https://doi.org/10.1007/s10961-006-0006-8

Peacock, Vita. 2016. "Academic Precarity as Hierarchical Dependence in the Max Planck Society." *HAU: Journal of Ethnographic Theory* 6(1): 95-119. https://doi.org/10.14318/hau6.1.006

Pink, Sarah. 2021. "The Ethnographic Hunch." In *Experimenting with Ethnography: A Companion to Analysis*, edited by Andrea Ballestero and Brit Ross Winthereik, pp. 30-40. Durham, NC: Duke University Press. https://doi.org/10.1215/9781478013211-004

Rothaermel, Frank T., and Marie Thursby. 2005. "University–Incubator Firm Knowledge Flows: Assessing Their Impact on Incubator Firm Performance." *Research Policy* 34(3): 305-20. https://doi.org/10.1016/j.respol.2004.11.006

Rutherford, Danilyn. 2012. "Kinky Empiricism." *Cultural Anthropology* 27(3): 465-79. https://doi.org/10.1111/j.1548-1360.2012.01154.x

Sarasvathy, Saras D. 2009. *Effectuation: Elements of Entrepreneurial Expertise*. Cheltenham, UK: Edward Elgar.

Shane, Scott. 2004. "Encouraging University Entrepreneurship? The Effect of the Bayh-Dole Act on University Patenting in the United States." *Journal of Business Venturing* 19(1): 127-51. https://doi.org/10.1016/S0883-9026(02)00114-3

Sicart, Miguel. 2014. *Play Matters*. Cambridge, MA: MIT Press.

Siegel, Donald S., and Mike Wright. 2015. "Academic Entrepreneurship: Time for a Rethink?." *British Journal of Management* 26(4): 582-95. https://doi.org/10.1111/1467-8551.12116

Shepherd, Dean A., and Holger Patzelt. 2018. *Entrepreneurial Cognition: Exploring the Mindset of Entrepreneurs*. Cham, Switzerland: Palgrave MacMillan/Springer Nature.

Stel, André van, Martin Carree, and Roy Thurik. 2005. "The Effect of Entrepreneurial Activity on National Economic Growth." *Small Business Economics* 24(3): 311-21. https://doi.org/10.1007/s11187-005-1996-6

Sunderland, Patricia L., and Rita M. Denny. 2003. "Psychology vs. Anthropology: Where Is Culture in Marketplace Ethnography." In *Advertising Cultures*, edited by Timothy de Waal Malefyt and Brian Moeran, pp. 187-202. New York: Routledge.

Van Holm, Eric Joseph. 2015. "Makerspaces and Contributions to Entrepreneurship." *Procedia-Social and Behavioral Sciences* 195: 24-31. https://doi.org/10.1016/j.sbspro.2015.06.167

Wolcott, Harry F. 2005. *The Art of Fieldwork*. Walnut Grove, CA: Rowman Altamira.

Wong, Bernard P. 1995. *Ethnicity and Etrepreneurship: The New Chinese Immigrants in the San Francisco Bay Area*. Boston: Allyn and Bacon.

Wright, Mike. 2007. *Academic Entrepreneurship in Europe*. Cheltenham, UK: Edward Elgar.

Zemeckis, Robert. 1997. *Contact*. 1997. Warner Bros.

Entrepreneurship in the "New Normal": Pandemic Ruptures and Continuities among Agra's Tourism Entrepreneurs
Riddhi Bhandari

Al Jazeera. 2021. "Taj Mahal Reopens for Tourists as India Eases COVID Curbs." June 16, 2021. https://www.aljazeera.com/news/2021/6/16/taj-mahal-reopens-for-tourists-as-india-eases-covid-curbs. Accessed January 12, 2022.

Anjaria, Jonathan. 2006. "Street Hawkers and Public Space in Mumbai." *Economic and Political Weekly* 41: 2140–46. https://www.jstor.org/stable/i401724

Bhandari, Riddhi. 2017. "Debts and Uncertainty: Circulation of Advance Money among Tourism Entrepreneurs in Agra, India." *Research in Economic Anthropology* 37: 233–56.

Bhandari, Riddhi. 2021. "Talking Crime and Aggression: Tourism and Governance in Agra, India." *South Asia: Journal of South Asian Studies* 44(4):721–38. https://doi.org/10.1080/00856401.2021.1941524

Cross, Jamie. 2010. "Neoliberalism as Unexceptional: Economic Zones and the Everyday Precariousness of Working Life in South India." *Critique of Anthropology* 30(4): 355–73. https://doi.org/10.1177/0308275X10372467

Datta, Damyanti. 2018. "Losing the Taj: Fighting a Monumental Neglect." *India Today*. July 21, 2018. https://www.indiatoday.in/magazine/cover-story/story/20180730-losing-the-taj-1289803-2018-07-21. Accessed January 12, 2022.

Divya, A. 2020. "Taj Mahal to Reopen after 6 Months, Cap of 5,000 Daily Visitors." *The Indian Express*. September 9, 2020. https://indianexpress.com/article/india/taj-mahal-to-reopen-after-6-months-cap-of-5000-daily-visitors/. Accessed January 12, 2022.

Ferguson, James, and Akhil Gupta. 2002. "Spatializing States: Toward an Ethnography of Neoliberal Governmentality." *American Ethnologist* 29(4): 981–1002. https://doi.org/10.1525/ae.2002.29.4.981

Galemba, Rebecca B. 2008. "Informal and Illicit Entrepreneurs: Fighting for a Place in the Neoliberal Economic Order." *Anthropology of Work Review* 29(2): 19–25. https://doi.org/10.1111/j.1548-1417.2008.00010.x

Ghosh, Ipshita. 2020. "Investment, Value, and the Making of Entrepreneurship in India." *Economic Anthropology* 7: 190–202. https://doi.org/10.1002/sea2.12179

Gupta, Akhil and Sivaramakrishnan, K., eds. 2011. *The State in India After Liberalization: Interdisciplinary Perspectives*. New York: Routledge.

Irani, Lilly. 2019. *Chasing Innovation: Making Entrepreneurial Citizens in Modern India*. Princeton, NJ: Princeton University Press.

Jeffrey, Craig, and Stephen Young. 2014. "Jugad: Youth and Enterprise in India." *Annals of The Association of American Geographers* 104(1): 182–95. https://doi.org/10.1080/00045608.2013.847757

Waters, Anita, M. 2003. "Heritage Tourism Development and Unofficial History in Port Royal, Jamaica." *Social and Economic Studies* 52(2): 1–27. https://www.jstor.org/stable/27865327

REFERENCES

In Pursuit of Quality and Taste: Post-Industrial Entrepreneurs
Atak Ayaz

Biron, Marcel. 1948. *Avrupa Üzüm Cinslerinin Türkiye (Trakya) Iklimine Intibaklari Acclimatation Des Cepages Europeens En Turquie (Thrace) 1937 à 1947*. Istanbul.

Bourdieu, Pierre. 1986. "The Forms of Capital." In *Handbook of Theory and Research for the Sociology of Education*, edited by John G. Richardson. New York: Greenwood Press.

Corti, Carlo. 2017. "Wine and Vineyards in the Hittite Kingdom: A Case Study of Northern Anatolia and the Southern Black Sea Coast." In *Of Vines and Wines: The Production and Consumption of Wine in Anatolian Civilizations through the Ages*, edited by Thys-Şenocak Lucienne. Leuven: Peeters.

Doğruel Fatma, and Doğruel A. Suut. 2000. *Osmanlı'dan Günümüze Tekel*. İstanbul: Türkiye Ekonomik ve Toplumsal Tarih Vakfı.

Eldem, Edhem. 2017. "A French View of the Ottoman-Turkish Wine Market, 1890-1925." In *Of Vines and Wines: The Production and Consumption of Wine in Anatolian Civilizations through the Ages*, edited by Thys-Şenocak Lucienne. Leuven: Peeters.

Halenko, Oleksandr. 2017. "Wine in the Public Discourse and Banqueting Practices of the Early Ottomans." In *Of Vines and Wines: The Production and Consumption of Wine in Anatolian Civilizations through the Ages*, edited by Thys-Şenocak Lucienne. Leuven: Peeters.

Jung, Yuson. 2016. "Re-Creating Economic and Cultural Values in Bulgaria's Wine Industry: From an Economy of Quantity to an Economy of Quality?" *Economic Anthropology* 3(2): 280–92. https://doi.org/10.1002/sea2.12057.

Paxson, Heather. 2013, *The Life of Cheese Crafting Food and Value in America*. Berkeley: University of California Press.

Simpson, James. 2011. *Creating Wine: The Emergence of a World Industry, 1840-1914*. Princeton, NJ: Princeton University Press.

Soileau, Mark. 2017. "A Vinicultural History of Tur 'Abdin." In *Of Vines and Wines: The Production and Consumption of Wine in Anatolian Civilizations through the Ages*, edited by Thys-Şenocak Lucienne. Leuven: Peeters.

Trubek, Amy B. 2008. *The Taste of Place: A Cultural Journey into Terroir*. Berkeley, CA: University of California Press.

Ulin, Robert C. 1996. *Vintages and Traditions: An Ethnohistory of Southwest French Wine Cooperatives*. Washington, DC: Smithsonian Institution Press.

Yanagisako, Sylvia Junko. 2002. *Producing Culture and Capital: Family Firms in Italy*. Princeton: Princeton University Press.

Pitching Hype: Storytelling and Entrepreneurship
Angela K. VandenBroek

Blank, Steve. 2013. "Steve Blank: The 6 Types of Startups." *The Accelerators (blog). Wall Street Journal*. June 24, 2013. https://blogs.wsj.com/accelerators/2013/06/24/steve-blank-the-6-types-of-startups-2/.

Blank, Steve, and Bob Dorf. 2012. *The Startup Owner's Manual: The Step-by-Step Guide for Building a Great Company*. BookBaby.

Brown, Nik. 2003. "Hope Against Hype - Accountability in Biopasts, Presents and Futures." *Science & Technology Studies* 16 (2): 3–21. https://doi.org/10.23987/sts.55152

Easterbrook, Steve. 2014. "From Computational Thinking to Systems Thinking: A Conceptual Toolkit for Sustainability Computing." In *Proceedings of the 2nd International Conference on Information and Communication Technologies for Sustainability (ICT 4S'2014).*

Fenn, Jackie, and Mark Raskino. 2008. *Mastering the Hype Cycle: How to Choose the Right Innovation at the Right Time.* Boston, MA: Harvard Business Press.

Frier, Sarah, and Eric Newcomer. 2015. "The Fuzzy, Insane Math That's Creating So Many Billion-Dollar Tech Companies." *Bloomberg News*, March 17, 2015. https://www.bloomberg.com/news/articles/2015-03-17/the-fuzzy-insane-math-that-s-creating-so-many-billion-dollar-tech-companies.

Hand, Martin, and Barry Sandywell. 2002. "E-Topia as Cosmopolis or Citadel: On the Democratizing and De-Democratizing Logics of the Internet, Or, Toward a Critique of the New Technological Fetishism." *Theory, Culture & Society* 19(1-2): 197–225. https://doi.org/10.1177/026327640201900110

Köhn, Andreas. 2018. "The Determinants of Startup Valuation in the Venture Capital Context: A Systematic Review and Avenues for Future Research." *Management Review Quarterly* 68(1): 3–36. https://doi.org/10.1007/s11301-017-0131-5

Lente, Harro van. 2012. "Navigating Foresight in a Sea of Expectations: Lessons from the Sociology of Expectations." *Technology Analysis & Strategic Management* 24(8): 769–82.

Maturo, Antonio. 2014. "Fatism, Self-Monitoring and the Pursuit of Healthiness in the Time of Technological Solutionism." *Italian Sociological Review* 4(2): 157–71.

Miloud, Tarek, Arild Aspelund, and Mathieu Cabrol. 2012. "Startup Valuation by Venture Capitalists: An Empirical Study." *Venture Capital* 14(2-3): 151–74. https://doi.org/10.1080/13691066.2012.667907

Morozov, E. 2013. *To Save Everything, Click Here: The Folly of Technological Solutionism.* New York: PublicAffairs.

Pink, Sarah, Katalin Osz, Kaspar Raats, Thomas Lindgren, and Vaike Fors. 2020. "Design Anthropology for Emerging Technologies: Trust and Sharing in Autonomous Driving Futures." *Design Studies* 69 (July): 100942. https://doi.org/10.1016/j.destud.2020.04.002

Poggiali, Lisa. 2016. "Seeing (from) Digital Peripheries: Technology and Transparency in Kenya's Silicon Savannah." *Cultural Anthropology* 31(3): 387–411. https://doi.org/10.14506/ca31.3.07

Powers, Devon. 2011. "Bruce Springsteen, Rock Criticism, and the Music Business: Towards a Theory and History of Hype." *Popular Music & Society* 34(2): 203–19. https://doi.org/10.1080/03007761003726472

Rajan, Kaushik Sunder. 2006. *Biocapital: The Constitution of Postgenomic Life.* Durham, NC: Duke University Press.

Röhm, Patrick, Andreas Köhn, Andreas Kuckertz, and Hermann S. Dehnen. 2018. "A World of Difference? The Impact of Corporate Venture Capitalists' Investment Motivation on Startup Valuation." *Journal of Business Economics and Management* 88(3): 531–57. https://doi.org/10.1007/s11573-017-0857-5

Segal, H. P. 1985. *Technological Utopianism in American Culture.* Syracuse, NY: Syracuse University Press.

Tiso, Giovanni. 2013. "'The Net Will Save Us': Political Solutionism and the Five Star Movement." *Overland* 211: 55–60.

Turner, F. 2010. *From Counterculture to Cyberculture: Stewart Brand, the Whole Earth Network, and the Rise of Digital Utopianism*. Chicago: University of Chicago Press.

Growth Hacking: On the Social Dimensions of High-Leverage Growth in Venture Capitalism
Jamie Wong

Bear, Laura. 2016. "Time as Technique." *Annual Review of Anthropology* 45: 487–502. https://doi.org/10.1146/annurev-anthro-102313-030159

Coleman, Gabriella. 2012. *Coding Freedom: The Ethics and Aesthetics of Hacking*. Princeton, NJ: Princeton University Press.

Coleman, Gabriella. 2014. *Hacker, Hoaxer, Whistleblower, Spy: The Many Faces of Anonymous*. Brooklyn, NY: Verso Books.

Fong, Raymond, and Chad Riddersen. 2017. *Growth Hacking: Silicon Valley's Best Kept Secret*. Austin, TX: Lioncrest Publishing.

Fortune, Reo. 1932. *Sorcerers of Dobu: The Social Anthropology of the Dobu Islanders of the Western Pacific*. New York: Routledge.

Fourcade, Marion, and Kieran Healy. 2017. "Seeing Like a Market." *Socio-Economic Review* 15 (1): 9–29. https://doi.org/10.1093/ser/mww033

Geertz, Clifford. 1963. *Peddlers and Princes: Social Development and Economic Change in Two Indonesian Towns*. Vol. 318. Chicago: University of Chicago Press.

Gell, Alfred. 2000. "Time and Social Anthropology." In *Time in Contemporary Intellectual Thought*, edited by Patrick Baert, 251–68. New York: Elsevier.

Granovetter, Mark S. 1973. "The Strength of Weak Ties." *American Journal of Sociology* 78 (6): 1360–80. https://doi.org/10.1086/225469

Guyer, Jane I. 2007. "Prophecy and the Near Future: Thoughts on Macroeconomic, Evangelical, and Punctuated Time." *American Ethnologist* 34 (3): 409–21. https://doi.org/10.1525/ae.2007.34.3.409

Helm, Sabrina, Kerstin Liehr-Gobbers, and Christopher Storck. 2011. *Reputation Management*. New York: Springer Science & Business Media.

Kipnis, Andrew. 1997. *Producing Guanxi: Sentiment, Self, and Subculture in a North China Village*. Durham, NC: Duke University Press.

Miller, Daniel. 1998. "Conclusion: A Theory of Virtualism." *Virtualism: A New Political Economy*, 187–215. Oxford: Berg.

Moore, Henrietta L. 2004. "Global Anxieties: Concept-Metaphors and Pre-Theoretical Commitments in Anthropology." *Anthropological Theory* 4 (1): 71–88. https://doi.org/10.1177%2F1463499604040848

Nicholas, Tom. 2019. *VC: An American History*. Cambridge, MA: Harvard University Press.

Sadowski, Jathan. 2019. "When Data Is Capital: Datafication, Accumulation, and Extraction." *Big Data & Society* 6 (1): 1–12. https://doi.org/10.1177%2F2053951718820549

Tsing, Anna Lowenhaupt. 2012. "On Nonscalability: The Living World Is Not Amenable to Precision-Nested Scales." *Common Knowledge* 18 (3): 505–24. https://doi.org/10.1215/0961754X-1630424

West, Sarah Myers. 2019. "Data Capitalism: Redefining the Logics of Surveillance and Privacy." *Business & Society* 58 (1): 20–41. https://doi.org/10.1177%2F0007650317718185

Xiang, Biao. 2020. "The Gyroscope-Like Economy: Hypermobility, Structural Imbalance and Pandemic Governance in China." *Inter-Asia Cultural Studies* 21 (4): 521–32. https://doi.org/10.1080/14649373.2020.1832305

Yan, Yunxiang. 1996. *The Flow of Gifts: Reciprocity and Social Networks in a Chinese Village*. Redwood City, CA: Stanford University Press.

Yang, Mayfair Mei-hui. 1994. *Gifts, Favors, and Banquets. The Art of Social Relationships in China*. Ithaca, NY: Cornell University Press.

Zuboff, Shoshana. 2019. *The Age of Surveillance Capitalism: The Fight for a Human Future at the New Frontier of Power*. London: Profile.

Entrepreneurship: A Dialogue with 2021 Symposium Authors
Patricia Sunderland, Atak Ayaz, Riddhi Bhandari, Matthew Hill, and Jamie Wong

Bear, Laura. 2014a. "Capital and Time: Uncertainty and Qualitative Measures of Inequality." *The British Journal of Sociology* 65 (4): 639–49. https://doi.org/10.1111/1468-4446.12107

Bear, Laura. 2014b. "For Labour: Ajeet's Accident and the Ethics of Technological Fixes in Time." *Journal of the Royal Anthropological Institute* 20: 71–88. https://doi.org/10.1111/1467-9655.12094

Bolton, Ralph, Jhuver Aguirre-Torres, and Ken C. Erickson. 2019. "Cheese in Chijnaya: Communal Entrepreneurship in Rural Peru." *Journal of Business Anthropology* 8(2):185–210. https://doi.org/10.22439/jba.v8i2.5848

Bourdieu, Pierre. 1977. *Outline of a Theory of Practice*. Translated by Richard Nice. Cambridge, UK: Cambridge University Press.

Bourdieu, Pierre. 2018. *The Forms of Capital*. New York: Routledge.

Clamp, Christina A., and Innocentus Alhamis. 2010. "Social Entrepreneurship in the Mondragon Co-Operative Corporation and the Challenges of Successful Replication." *The Journal of Entrepreneurship* 19(2):149–77. https://doi.org/10.1177%2F097135571001900204

Fortune, Reo. 1932. *Sorcerers of Dobu: The Social Anthropology of the Dobu Islanders of the Western Pacific*. London: Routledge.

Geertz, Clifford. 1963. *Peddlers and Princes: Social Development and Economic Change in Two Indonesian Towns*. Chicago: University of Chicago Press.

Guyer, Jane I, and Samuel M Eno Belinga. 1995. "Wealth in People as Wealth in Knowledge: Accumulation and Composition in Equatorial Africa." *The Journal of African History* 36(1): 91–120. doi:10.1017/S0021853700026992

MacKenzie, Donald A, Fabian Muniesa, and Lucia Siu, eds. 2008. *Do Economists Make Markets?: On the Performativity of Economics*. Princeton, NJ: Princeton University Press.

Nelms, Taylor C., and Stephen C. Rea. 2019. *The Credit Union of the Twenty-First Century*. 459. Madison, WI: Filene Research Institute.

Osburg, John. 2013. *Anxious Wealth. Money and Morality Among China's New Rich*. Redwood City, CA: Stanford University Press.

Paxson, Heather. 2013. *The Life of Cheese Crafting Food and Value in America*. Berkeley: University of California Press.

Riles, Annelise. 2011. *Collateral Knowledge: Legal Reasoning in the Global Financial Markets*. Chicago: University of Chicago Press.

Ringel, Felix. 2016. "Can Time Be Tricked?: A Theoretical Introduction." *The Cambridge Journal of Anthropology* 34 (1): 22–31. https://doi.org/10.3167/ca.2016.340104

Schumpeter, J.A. 1934. *The Theory of Economic Development*. Cambridge, MA: Harvard University Press.

Tsing, Anna Lowenhaupt. 2012. "On Nonscalability: The Living World Is Not Amenable to Precision-Nested Scales." *Common Knowledge* 18(3): 505–24. https://doi.org/10.1215/0961754X-1630424

Uretsky, Elanah. 2016. *Occupational Hazards: Sex, Business, and HIV in Post-Mao China*. Redwood City, CA: Stanford University Press.